GOD'S GALS

Haven't Changed A Bit!

Lynnelle Pierce

Lynnelle Pierce
928 Sand Lake Drive
Zeeland, MI 49464
©1997 Lynnelle Pierce
Second printing May, 1999
Third printing March, 2001

Unless otherwise indicated, "Scripture taken from the HOLY BIBLE: NEW INTERNATIONAL VERSION®. NIV®. Copyright© 1973, 1978, 1984 by International Bible Society. Used by permission of Zondervan Publishing House." "The "NIV" and "New International Version" trademarks are registered in the United States Patent and Trademark Office by International Bible Society."

Scripture quotations marked (KJV) are taken from the King James Version of the Bible.

Cover Design: Michael A. Vander Wall
Cover Photographer: Nick de Vries
Editing: George Jasperse, Jon Mulder
Legal: William Dani

Lynnelle Pierce and her husband Tom
live in Zeeland, Michigan
and are the parents of two grown sons.
Their home church
titles them missionaries
as they go out from one coast to the other
sharing their faith
in that wonderfully old
but life-changing story of Jesus.
Their pure, genuine, and simple approach
through Lynnelle's singing at concerts,
her speaking at conferences,
and the Bible studies she teaches
affects all ages,
from the children to the elderly.
She believes the Gospel has a powerful way
of doing that.
Lynnelle has a way of writing
the way she talks—
straight from her heart.
That was one of the most repeated comments
made about her first book,
Have You Heard About That Fruit?
She followed with
that same touch in
God's Gals Haven't Changed a Bit!
You will see that both of her books
are totally based on
the very principles of God's Holy Word.
She wouldn't have it
any other way.

Take time
to step out of your Reeboks
and into the sandals
of women from the Word.
Surprisingly enough,
their journey is our journey—
full of twists, turns, valleys, and vistas.
Lynnelle joins us
in the journey
pointing out the paths, pitfalls and peaks.
Thanks Lynnelle—
what a grand adventure!
And you are right,
God's Gals Haven't Changed a Bit!

Patsy Clairmont

I dedicate this book
to two very special people, who,
just at the right time—
God's time—
came into our lives
to help us take this ministry
to a new level
and reach out to many more people.
Martin and Kay Den Braber,
thank you for allowing the Lord
to use you and the gifts
that He's given you
and combine them with mine
to make these books possible.
I know,
all for the glory of God, right?
Yes,
but I'll always be grateful
for your beautiful servant hearts.

TABLE OF CONTENTS

Introduction

Your word, O Lord, is eternal; it stands firm in the heavens. Your faithfulness continues through all generations; you established the earth, and it endures (Psalm 119:89-90).

Recently, a survey was taken on the religious pulse of our nation.[1] The results were startling. "Nine out of 10 Americans own a Bible, but fewer than half read it." The inspired Word of God is not being used for instruction, guidance, and spiritual growth in the way the Lord intended according to II Timothy 3:16-17.

All Scripture is God-breathed and is useful for teaching, rebuking, correcting and training in righteousness, so that the man of God may be thoroughly equipped for every good work.

The survey listed three "reasons for lack of Bible reading: (1) Don't have time, (2) Too hard to understand, and (3) Not relevant to their lives."

I was not surprised with the first reason given. Life is jammed full; and because there is so much that "must get done," people push God's Word aside—the very words that would sustain them during their hectic schedules. Unfortunately, they are the ones who don't have a clue that the Bible is really alive and exciting. His Book brings strength and comfort; it gives the best instruction for experiencing life abundantly and to the fullest. The Bible is the greatest "how to" book on marriage, making decisions, and raising children. I could go on and on, but I think you get the point. Such people are avoiding the very answers to life that they desperately seek. It's all right there in The Book. They just have to choose to take the time to read it. I'm afraid there are too many who do not believe that God's Word does have the answers. No time? That is a sad commentary on the importance of God in their lives.

The second reason: "Too hard to understand," is a convenient excuse. Of course they do not understand it on their own; no one does—at least not merely with a human brain. It also requires the heart. Heart understanding of Scripture, however, can only come from the Holy Spirit. He is here in the hearts of His people to help them understand and guide them into all truth.

We have not received the spirit of the world but the Spirit who is from God, that we may understand what God has freely given us. This is what we speak, not in words taught us by human wisdom but in words taught by the Spirit, expressing spiritual truths in spiritual words. The man without the Spirit does not accept the things that come from the Spirit of God, for they are foolishness to him, and he cannot understand them, because they are spiritually discerned (I Corinthians 2:12-14).

This leads to a very important question: "Do you know that the Holy Spirit dwells within your heart?" That's right! You can know it. If you do not know it, I am certain that the verses you just read made no sense to you at all. Now read these life-changing words from Paul in Romans 8:9-11:

You, however, are controlled not by the sinful nature but by the Spirit, if the Spirit of God lives in you. And if anyone does not have the Spirit of Christ, he does not belong to Christ. But if Christ is in you, your body is dead because of sin, yet your spirit is alive because of righteousness. And if the Spirit of him who raised Jesus from the dead is living in you, he who raised Christ from the dead will also give life to your mortal bodies through his Spirit, who lives in you.

You see, it doesn't have to be complicated. You can have Jesus' very Spirit living inside your heart making understanding possible. Simply profess Jesus as your only Savior, invite Him to live in your heart (He's just been waiting for your invitation), repent of your sins, and ask Him to help you change your ways. How exciting to hear this in II Corinthians 5:17:

> *Therefore, if anyone is in Christ, he is a new creation; the old has gone, the new has come!*

Believe that Jesus' death and resurrection were for YOU, and then you will receive His Holy Spirit. Watch a new you unfold!

> *Now it is God who makes both us and you stand firm in Christ. He anointed us, set his seal of ownership on us, and put his Spirit in our hearts as a deposit, guaranteeing what is to come (II Corinthians 1:21-22).*

You can KNOW and UNDERSTAND! It is right there before your very eyes from God's holy Word. Hold on; your eyes are now opening. It is no wonder that when John Newton realized the amazing grace of God, he wrote, "I was blind, but now I see."[2]

Oh, boy, do I see! Everyday, when I study God's Word and ask the Holy Spirit to illuminate the words on the page, I "see" more.

After a Bible study one day, a dear woman asked me what it was like sitting on the leader's stool and having the privilege of watching "lights" (of understanding) come on in the faces of the women. My answer came quickly. I replied, "There is something very special about being able to literally watch and see the Holy Spirit do His job. That is what He promised to do in each individual who allows Him to do it. Yes, I am in a very privileged position—watching our God at work in their lives and mine."

Finally, the third reason why the Bible is not read is the very reason this book was written. The Bible is "not relevant to their lives," some say! Let me take you into the Old Testament and introduce, or reintroduce you to Eve, Sarah, Hagar, Miriam, Rahab, Ruth, Naomi, Hannah, Abigail, the Shunammite woman, Esther, and from the New Testament, Mary and several others. Do you know what you are going to see? You guessed it! "God's Gals Haven't Changed a Bit!," and His ways of dealing with us haven't changed either. The verse at the beginning of this introduction says it:

> *Your word, O Lord, is eternal; it stands firm in the heavens (Psalm 119:89).*

Hang on! You're in for a ride. A ride that will prove that the Bible is right on course, just as it was thousands of years ago.

1

EVE

Eve was the first woman. Many of us have heard the creation story many times: on the sixth day, God made man in His own image *from the dust of the ground and breathed into his nostrils the breath of life, and the man became a living being* (Genesis 2:7). After having Adam name all the animals and birds, the Lord could see that Adam needed a suitable helper. So, He caused Adam to fall into a deep sleep, removed a rib from his side, and made a woman. Did you notice it was not from Adam's head to rule over her, or from his feet to walk over her? But rather, I like to think God took the rib from under man's arm to protect, love, and hold the woman close to his heart.

They lived in total perfection. That is entirely beyond our comprehension because you and I have been conceived in sin.

Surely I was sinful at birth, sinful from the time my mother conceived me (Psalm 51:5).

Everything we see today is tainted by sin. But at the beginning of time, all was blissful perfection. When we read Genesis 2, we cannot help but wonder why it could not have stayed that way. How quickly that is answered by a mere turn of the page to Genesis 3.

Knowing that Eve lived in perfection and that life could not get any better, we would think that Satan had his hands full trying to come up with a master scheme that would cause the fall of mankind. He knew exactly what avenue to take, however: plant a seed of DOUBT in her mind. She'd take it from there.

Where did Satan come from, anyway, in that glorious, perfect world? He had fallen out of heaven.

> *How art thou fallen from heaven, O Lucifer, son of the morning! (Isaiah 14:12a KJV).*

Yes, he was once one of God's angels, but because of his "control" problem (not wanting to submit to Almighty God and desiring instead to share our Lord's glory), he was booted out of heaven.

> *"I am the Lord; that is my name! I will not give my glory to another or my praise to idols" (Isaiah 42:8).*

Following that, his goal was to control earth and everything and everyone who lived there. Read how his plan unfolds in Genesis 3:1-13.

> *Now the serpent was more crafty than any of the wild animals the Lord God*

had made. He said to the woman, "Did God really say, 'You must not eat from any tree in the garden'?"

The woman said to the serpent, "We may eat fruit from the trees in the garden, but God did say, 'You must not eat fruit from the tree that is in the middle of the garden, and you must not touch it, or you will die.'"

"You will not surely die," the serpent said to the woman. "For God knows that when you eat of it your eyes will be opened, and you will be like God, knowing good and evil."

When the woman saw that the fruit of the tree was good for food and pleasing to the eye, and also desirable for gaining wisdom, she took some and ate it. She also gave some to her husband, who was with her, and he ate it. Then the eyes of both of them were opened, and they realized they were naked; so they sewed fig leaves together and made coverings for themselves.

Then the man and his wife heard the sound of the Lord God as he was walking in the garden in the cool of the day, and they hid from the Lord God among the trees of the garden. But the Lord God called to the man, "Where are you?"

> *He answered, "I heard you in the garden, and I was afraid because I was naked; so I hid."*
>
> *And he said, "Who told you that you were naked? Have you eaten from the tree that I commanded you not to eat from?"*
>
> *The man said, "The woman you put here with me—she gave me some fruit from the tree, and I ate it."*
>
> *Then the Lord God said to the woman, "What is this you have done?"*
>
> *The woman said, "The serpent deceived me, and I ate."*

Satan was smart and still is, because he hasn't changed a bit. He lied, deceived, and was downright conniving. He was full of poisonous venom. His prey was an innocent woman, and his plan was to create doubt and discontent.

Satan came in the form of a serpent. He was probably walking because it was not until after the fall that God cursed him to crawl on his belly. Did animals talk? The Bible does not explain that. But it is very clear that Eve and the serpent communicated and understood each other as plain as could be. There must have been a great rapport between man and animal at that time.

The serpent, being more crafty than any of the wild animals (Genesis 3:1), asked Eve, *"Did God really say, 'You must not eat from any tree in the garden'?"* That was the question that changed everything. Eve knew full well the command of the Lord in Genesis 2:16-17:

And the Lord God commanded the man,
"You are free to eat from any tree in the
garden; but you must not eat from the tree
of the knowledge of good and evil, for when
you eat of it you will surely die."

It could not have been stated any clearer than that. At that moment, Eve should have responded in full force saying: "God said it and that settles it." Yet the power of doubt made that clear command from God questionable. The same tree that was absolutely forbidden, now definitely had more appeal after looking at it through Satan's eyes. Yes, in fact, it looked good and pleasing to Eve, and her desire to gain knowledge was tremendous. The serpent's fangs struck. The venom started to poison the mind and body.

The temptation was not the sin. It never is. We have a way out—God's way. When tempted, we have a conscious choice to make. See it in I Corinthians 10:13:

No temptation has seized you except what is
common to man. And God is faithful; he
will not let you be tempted beyond what you
can bear. But when you are tempted, he
will also provide a way out so that you can
stand up under it.

If we do not choose to go to Him for our way out, the temptation presented to us then turns into an action—sin. James 1:13-15 reminds us:

*When tempted, no one should say, "God is
tempting me." For God cannot be tempted
by evil, nor does he tempt anyone; but each
one is tempted when, by his own evil desire,
he is dragged away and enticed. Then, after
desire has conceived, it gives birth to sin;
and sin, when it is full-grown, gives birth to
death.*

Eve's series of events went like this: once Satan
had his fangs in her, she listened, looked, took, ate, and
then gave the fruit to Adam. At any time during that
series of events, she could (and should) have turned to
her God for help—He was right there.

*The Lord is righteous in all his ways and
loving toward all he has made. The Lord is
near to all who call on him, to all who call
on him in truth (Psalm 145:17-18).*

Oh, but before we put all the blame on Eve,
reread Genesis 3:6. Yes, you read it right. Adam was
right there with her. That is why blaming each other was
actually quite ridiculous. Each of them had a choice to
make and could have called out to their God.

On the subject of making choices, I am reminded
of the story of Joseph and Potiphar's wife from
Genesis 39. Joseph was the son of Jacob. He had
brothers who were jealous of him; they sold him to the
Ishmaelites, who then took him to Egypt. Because God
was with Joseph and had a very unique plan for him, this

Israelite ended up as the head of Potiphar's household. Potiphar was one of Pharaoh's officials and the captain of the guard.

> *Now Joseph was well-built and handsome, and after a while his master's wife took notice of Joseph and said, "Come to bed with me!" (v.6b-7)*

> *And though she spoke to Joseph day after day, he refused to go to bed with her or even be with her.*
> *One day he went into the house to attend to his duties, and none of the household servants was inside. She caught him by his cloak and said, "Come to bed with me!" But he left his cloak in her hand and ran out of the house (v.10-12).*

He handled the temptation perfectly. He ran. When we feel ourselves being tempted, get out! He had the perfect answer, too. He said, *"How then could I do such a wicked thing and sin against God?" (v.9c)*

If Adam and Eve had just done that, what a different world it would be. If we would just do what Joseph did, how different we would be.

Adam and Eve succumbed to the devil's temptation, however, and instantly there were consequences. SELF was born—you know, the "me, myself, and I" syndrome. What a pity! They were immediately separated from God. That was the ultimate consequence; that is exactly what sin does. The relationship between God and man was broken. They suddenly realized they were naked. Why? Because they had a new awareness of each other and their shame.

They also experienced feelings they had never felt before. They now knew what it felt like to feel guilty and to feel the hold of Satan's grip through fear. Then, of course, came blame (it is still the classic excuse today). Rather than accepting responsibility for our actions, we blame others.

Adam and Eve each blatantly disobeyed God's command. All through the Bible it is very evident that God takes sin very seriously; He will not put up with it. ALL sin will be dealt with either by Jesus' blood or God's judgment, and here we see the beginnings of grace. God sought Adam and Eve out and asked, *"Where are you?"* He had the right to end their lives, and they deserved to drop dead on the spot. We now start to experience His unexplainable, unconditional love for mankind.

Sin not only will be dealt with, but it also has its consequences. For Adam, Eve, and the serpent, the story continues in Genesis 3:14-19:

> *So the Lord God said to the serpent,*
> *"Because you have done this,*
>
> *"Cursed are you above all the livestock and all the wild animals! You will crawl on your belly and you will eat dust all the days of your life. And I will put*

enmity between you and the woman, and between your offspring and hers; he will crush your head, and you will strike his heel. "ৗ

To the woman he said,

"I will greatly increase your pains in childbearing; with pain you will give birth to children. Your desire will be for your husband, and he will rule over you. "

To Adam he said, "Because you listened to your wife and ate from the tree about which I commanded you, 'You must not eat of it,'

"Cursed is the ground because of you; through painful toil you will eat of it all the days of your life. It will produce thorns and thistles for you, and you will eat the plants of the field. By the sweat of your brow you will eat your food until you return to the ground, since from it you were taken; for dust you are and to dust you will return. "

The serpent was cursed. He would now crawl on his belly, eat dust, and in the end his head would be crushed.

Eve would experience pain (again, something new) in childbearing; and although before the fall there was no need for "positions," now man would rule over her.

Before the fall, work was wonderful and creative. Adam now would work and experience pain, suffering, and sweat.

There would be no more dwelling in earthly paradise, the Garden of Eden. No, they were sent out. Mankind would now die and return to the dust of the earth.

Maybe you're saying, "It was only one tree, only one piece of fruit." "What's the big deal?" "Why was the punishment so severe?" Let me tell you why: to God a sin is a sin. There are no big ones or little ones in His eyes.

For whoever keeps the whole law
and yet stumbles at just one point is guilty
of breaking all of it (James 2:10).

"James reminds us that if we've broken just one law, we are sinners. We can't decide to keep part of God's law and ignore the rest. You can't break the law a little bit; if you have broken it at all, you need Christ to pay for your sin. Measure yourself, not someone else, against God's standards."[3]

Adam and Eve's sin was sheer disobedience to God, and thus this one sin had worldwide effects on everyone. I repeat, sin is sin, and the ramifications can complicate and burden so many lives.

Although as severe and deserved as those consequences were, we see the gold thread Jesus began to weave. It might appear that when Jesus died on the cross Satan won (struck His heel), but when Jesus rose from the dead, He broke the power sin and death had over us and crushed Satan's head.

How do we fight back and not fall into Satan's traps? The answer remains the same—God's Word— constantly choosing to focus on our infallible God rather than on our fallible self. Also, knowing God's Word, listening to His Word, and being doers of His Word will always prepare us for life's choices.

Ephesians 6:10-18 shows us that we can (our choice) put on the whole armor of God—our most powerful weapon against Satan himself. The battle is real.

Finally, be strong in the Lord and in his mighty power. Put on the full armor of God so that you can take your stand against the devil's schemes. For our struggle is not against flesh and blood, but against the rulers, against the authorities, against the powers of this dark world and against the spiritual forces of evil in the heavenly realms. Therefore put on the full armor of God, so that when the day of evil comes, you may be able to stand your ground, and after you have done everything, to stand. Stand firm then, with the belt of truth buckled around your waist, with the

*breastplate of righteousness in place, and
with your feet fitted with the readiness that
comes from the gospel of peace. In addition
to all this, take up the shield of faith, with
which you can extinguish all the flaming
arrows of the evil one. Take the helmet of
salvation and the sword of the Spirit, which
is the word of God. And pray in the Spirit
on all occasions with all kinds of prayers
and requests. With this in mind, be alert
and always keep on praying for all the
saints.*

There are several distinct pieces of armor that the
Lord gives us to protect ourselves against the attacks of
Satan. The first one is the belt of truth. The more we
know the truth of our God and His Word, the more our
faith grows and the stronger the belt gets. That belt of
truth is the center of it all.

Second, the Lord gives us the breastplate of
righteousness to protect our heart; and yes, it needs
tender but firm protection. Our heart governs who we
really are. When we know, understand, and grasp the
fact that we have been made right by Jesus' sacrifice on
the cross, it changes our heart and our whole purpose for
living—we no longer live for ourselves, but we live to
bring glory to God.

Third, our feet must be ready and rock solid in the
Gospel—the best news of Jesus which gives us peace.

Fourth, in our hand we hold the shield of faith.
When our faith is firmly in place, we are steadfast and

can withstand the arrows of temptation that Satan throws at us.

The fifth piece of armor that we wear is the helmet of salvation to protect our mind. With our mind we constantly make choices to either follow our way or God's way. Continually choosing to know and accept that our salvation is only in Jesus makes us want God's way. Without our salvation, no matter how good a person we are, we are in a helplessly, hopelessly lost state. Our salvation should mean everything to us.

The sixth piece, the sword of the Spirit, is a powerful weapon for our use in battle. We use the sword—God's Word, the Bible—as our offensive and defensive weapon against our enemy. God's Word has a way of buckling Satan's schemes. Our prime example was Jesus. He used Scripture to win the "game" Satan tried to play with Him in Matthew 4:1-11. Remember, however, in order to use the sword for either fighting back or for protection, we have to know how to use it. And we really have to know that weapon thoroughly to be able to use it right. That's one more great reason for studying His Word every day.

And every day, it is essential that we pray. Prayer is what keeps God's heart connected to ours. We must never break that communication line.

Did you notice that there's no armor for the back? I would love to think it's because the Lord wants us to face our foe head on, never running from him. With the Lord and with the armor He gives us, no foe is too great. He doesn't leave us to battle any foe from Satan on our own. But we must choose daily to look to the Lord and

wear His armor into battle. The alternative is to face the
devil one-on-one. That leaves us helpless, because Satan
doesn't need much of a crack to slither through our
inadequate human armor to attack us. Keep in mind, that
is why Paul said to *be strong in the Lord* and *put on the
full armor of God.*

As I write this, I am reminded of what damage a
little crack in our armor can do. I was the Bible study
leader of a wonderful group of women. I had been their
leader for a number of years. It was our first week of
Bible study in the fall of the year after our summer
break. I was introducing them to our study for the year
and doing my best to convince them that Bible study is
very important. It changes us powerfully into people with
a Christ-like character, and I was trying to prove it to
them using Psalm 119.

> *v.9-11: How can a young man keep his way
> pure? By living according to your word. I
> seek you with all my heart; do not let me
> stray from your commands. I have hidden
> your word in my heart that I might not sin
> against you.*

> *v.18: Open my eyes that I may see
> wonderful things in your law.*

> *v.33-37: Teach me, O Lord, to follow your
> decrees; then I will keep them to the end.
> Give me understanding, and I will keep
> your law and obey it with all my heart.*

Direct me in the path of your commands, for there I find delight. Turn my heart toward your statutes and not toward selfish gain. Turn my eyes away from worthless things; preserve my life according to your word.

v.105: Your word is a lamp to my feet and a light for my path.

v.114: You are my refuge and my shield; I have put my hope in your word.

v.133: Direct my footsteps according to your word; let no sin rule over me.

v.175-176: Let me live that I may praise you, and may your laws sustain me. I have strayed like a lost sheep. Seek your servant, for I have not forgotten your commands.

I was on a roll. Everything was going great. They were listening, and the verses were speaking for themselves.

In this particular group of women there was a wide variety of ages, social standards, and knowledge of the Lord. In fact, many were new, and their training in God's Word was limited. So, as usual, I shared the plan of salvation. One can never assume that everyone in a particular gathering has experienced Jesus' salvation. Even with a bunch of "godly church women," there might be one who has been playing religion and church but never really asked Jesus to be her Lord and Savior. Maybe the Holy Spirit was still perched on her shoulder, whispering in her ear, drawing her to Jesus in a real and personal way.

> *"But when he, the Spirit of truth, comes, he will guide you into all truth. He will not speak on his own; he will speak only what he hears, and he will tell you what is yet to come. He will bring glory to me by taking from what is mine and making it known to you" (John 16:13-14).*

Just maybe she was hearing that still, small voice of the Holy Spirit, and this was the time she chose to listen and say yes to that Voice. Then the Holy Spirit would leave the perch on her shoulder and change residences—He would enter her heart.

As I was sharing the plan of salvation, however, everything started going a little crazy. As I looked out at all the women, suddenly that "power of doubt" thing went berserk. I told myself that they were probably thinking: "She has told us all of that before." "Oh, how boring; repeat, repeat, repeat." "Is that all she knows?" The power of doubt was taking root, and it was relentless. Satan knows that if he can get doubt-a-rolling, we will take it from there. I started to break out into a sweat. I got a tickle in my throat and started to choke. I was in the middle of a war and did not realize it. A morning that had started out so well was ending in disaster. I felt like a failure. Maybe it was time to quit. All of my feelings were going haywire because Satan planted one little seed of doubt in my mind. The study time came to a close, and I was very shaken.

As I got into my car and started on my way home, I was deeply troubled. About halfway home, the Lord's Spirit turned the lights of understanding on for me so I could see the truth. He helped me expose Satan for what he was trying to do to me.

Of course! That was it! Satan had created doubt to get me off the subject of salvation. He had tried to get me to believe that the old story of Jesus' love and sacrifice does get stale. That was a tempting, devilish lie! This salvation story gets better and better; I had caught Satan at his trickery, and it was over! "In Jesus Name, get lost!" I demanded. It was an extraordinary and victorious feeling all at the same time.

What a valuable, everyday, practical lesson for me to experience on doubt. Satan is the author of doubt—don't let him plant that seed in your mind. How can the mind recognize and reason with doubt? Listen to what Paul says in Romans 12:2:

> *Do not conform any longer to the pattern of this world, but be transformed by the renewing of your mind. Then you will be able to test and approve what God's will is—his good, pleasing and perfect will.*

Preach it Paul! Amen! He goes on in II Corinthians 10:5-6:

We demolish arguments and every pretension that sets itself up against the knowledge of God, and we take captive every thought to make it obedient to Christ. And we will be ready to punish every act of disobedience, once your obedience is complete.

Because of Jesus and His Word, I won and Satan lost. Praise the Lord!

So, Eve, thanks for the lesson. What a different world it would be if you would have gone to the Lord first. Oh, but then, that's the lesson for all of us, isn't it? When Satan dangles that bait in front of us, before he coils and strikes and his poisonous venom reaches our system, we have a tremendous power that we can choose to plug into—the very name of Jesus. The sound of a song, a Scripture verse, or a prayer, when done in Jesus' name, will force Satan to flee. Then we can resist our evil desire to submit to his temptation and enticing.

Temptations will always be near; the solution, in Jesus' name, will also always be near. The Lord is right here, waiting to help when we choose to ask Him—and we will find that His power has no limit.

A friend once told me that when my feet hit the floor in the morning, Satan himself must say, "Oh, no, she's up!" When I'm in tune with the Holy Spirit, Satan is one defeated foe—and I'm ready for one more powerful, exciting day with the Lord. Our potential is limitless.

As you finish reading this chapter, do you hear God asking you the same question He asked Adam and Eve after they sinned? Only you can answer when He asks, *"Where are you?"* Where is your heart today? Does God rule it? Does He have complete control? He wants nothing less.

Remember that because of sin there is physical death, but a heart without Jesus will experience spiritual death—hell. Those are the cold, hard facts. Can't you feel God's love when He asks you, *"Where are you?"* It is not His will that any perish (II Peter 3:9).

And finally, there are those of you who know you belong to the Lord, but you feel that Satan has a hold on you. Yes, he is the devil, the god of this world, the prince of darkness. But rest assured, he has only as much power over you as you let him have. John tells us in I John 4:4:

> *You, dear children, are from God and have overcome them* [the evil spirits of Satan], *because the one who is in you is greater than the one who is in the world.*

The battle's been won. Satan's head has been crushed. There is victory in Jesus. Victory in Jesus is hard to explain. It has to be experienced personally. I dare you to try it. It's marvelous!

2

SARAH

AND

HAGAR

There is a way that seems right to a man,
but in the end it leads to death
(Proverbs 14:12).

None of us wants to admit this, but if we are honest with ourselves, we realize there are times when we feel we had better help the Lord out with the plan He has for our lives. I don't know why we keep doing that; God's will for us is pleasing and perfect (Romans 12:2). I guess we just seem to forget that, especially when God's will causes us to wait, or when it goes against all human logic.

That's exactly how it was for Sarah. She felt she had waited long enough, even though she knew God had given the promise to Abraham that his descendants would number as many as the stars in the heavens (Genesis 15:5). But that had been years ago. Enough was enough. Watch her take matters into her own hands in Genesis 16:1-13.

Now Sarai, Abram's wife, had borne
him no children. But she had an Egyptian

*maidservant named Hagar; so she said to
Abram, "The Lord has kept me from having
children. Go, sleep with my maidservant;
perhaps I can build a family through her."*

*Abram agreed to what Sarai said. So
after Abram had been living in Canaan ten
years, Sarai his wife took her Egyptian
maidservant Hagar and gave her to her
husband to be his wife. He slept with
Hagar, and she conceived.*

*When she knew she was pregnant,
she began to despise her mistress. Then
Sarai said to Abram, "You are responsible
for the wrong I am suffering. I put my
servant in your arms, and now that she
knows she is pregnant, she despises me.
May the Lord judge between you and me."*

*"Your servant is in your hands,"
Abram said. "Do with her whatever you
think best." Then Sarai mistreated Hagar;
so she fled from her.*

*The angel of the Lord found Hagar
near a spring in the desert; it was the
spring that is beside the road to Shur. And
he said, "Hagar, servant of Sarai, where
have you come from, and where are you
going?"*

*"I'm running away from my mistress
Sarai," she answered.*

*Then the angel of the Lord told her,
"Go back to your mistress and submit to*

her." The angel added, "I will so increase your descendants that they will be too numerous to count."

The angel of the Lord also said to her:

"You are now with child and you will have a son. You shall name him Ishmael, for the Lord has heard of your misery. He will be a wild donkey of a man; his hand will be against everyone and everyone's hand against him, and he will live in hostility toward all his brothers."

She gave this name to the Lord who spoke to her: "You are the God who sees me," for she said, "I have now seen the One who sees me."

Everything got out of hand because all of the parties involved were out of God's will. I do feel sorry for Hagar, for she was a slave and had no voice in this plan at all.

I can see Sarah's logic, because having more than one wife was culturally permissible. It all sounds so reasonable, but there was one MAJOR problem. On this occasion, Sarah and Abraham failed to go to the Lord and ask for His direction. It is so hard to remember and fathom that God's timetable is not our timetable. When He says wait, He means wait—and they did not.

Sin reaps consequences. I'm certain that Sarah regretted her plan from the second Abraham left her tent for Hagar's. The thought of sharing my husband with another woman, culturally correct or not, is absurd. Just because "everybody is doing it" doesn't make it right. In Genesis 2:24, God gives this command:

> *For this reason a man will leave his father and mother and be united to his wife, and they will become one flesh.*

From this verse, it's clear that God never intended the ratio of men and women to be anything other than one to one. When that was disobeyed, problems were guaranteed to happen—and they did.

The plan was in motion, and Hagar conceived. Tables turned on Sarah as Hagar developed an attitude—a bit cocky. The slave girl now felt superior to her mistress because of her ability to get pregnant. When I saw this change in Hagar, I thought of these verses in Proverbs 6:16-19:

> *There are six things the Lord hates, seven that are detestable to him: haughty eyes, a lying tongue, hands that shed innocent blood, a heart that devises wicked schemes, feet that are quick to rush into evil, a false witness who pours out lies and a man who stirs up dissension among brothers.*

Yes, the Lord hates and detests these attitudes and characteristics. I know that is mighty strong language, but it is very obvious that the Lord means business.

Hagar's attitude obviously affected Sarah deeply. Sarah went to Abraham, who, in a rather cowardly manner, threw the problem back into her court. Sarah decided to mistreat Hagar to the point of Hagar's running away. They had a real mess there. It was out of control! Being out of God's will brings misery and chaos time and time again.

In spite of this, as demonstrated so many other times in the Old Testament, we see the Father's love and mercy when it is so undeserved. We see it here. The Lord met Hagar along the road in the desert—all alone. That is just like our loving Lord. He will meet us right where we are, because we could never attain His level. He takes us just as we are.

The Lord confronted her and gave her instruction. She must go back to Sarah and face the music—submit to her.

Hagar's returning to Sarah would be very humbling, but that is exactly what the Lord expected and desired. Humbling ourselves is difficult, but I love what happens when we do.

Humble yourselves before the Lord, and he will lift you up (James 4:10).

Why do we fight humbling ourselves when we read a verse like that? To be lifted up by our Lord to a higher plane than we could ever achieve sounds wonderful to me.

The Lord promised Hagar that her descendants would be too numerous to count. He also promised that she would have a son, Ishmael. But, because this was not a part of the covenant given to Abraham, there would be severe consequences. There would always be friction and hostility among his nation and others. (Ishmael's descendants are the Arabs of today. God's Word is true.)

Hagar was not a Jew, but because she served Abraham and Sarah in their home, it is likely she was well aware of the Jewish religion and customs. She might even have been involved with some of the formalities of the Jewish faith. But Hagar's faith was never personal until that moment when she acknowledged God. The personal relationship between her and her God had begun, and she would never be the same.

Hagar returned to Sarah and complied with God's command with a changed heart and attitude.

God does have a marvelous way of creating good out of our bad choices. He shows us that suffering brings us to the end of ourselves, because then we realize how desperately we need Him. But He never lets us get away with sin, and there will be consequences; yet His mercy and grace will forever sustain a repentant soul. His acceptance of us after we fail Him is truly beyond what our minds can comprehend. We cannot say thank You enough.

The key lesson from this story is WAIT. For me, waiting used to be one big waste of time. Now I see that the Lord is doing a mighty work in all parties involved when we wait. No wonder one of the fruit of His Spirit is patience, because it is impossible for us to develop it on our own. Such a fruit does not happen naturally. Only

His Spirit can work the words wait, forgive, and submit into our frail human state.

When we fail to wait for God, jump the gun, and try to "fix it" ourselves, we miss the very best God has for us. How do I know that? Read this:

But they that wait upon the Lord shall renew their strength; they shall mount up with wings as eagles; they shall run, and not be weary; and they shall walk, and not faint (Isaiah 40:31 KJV).

See what I mean? Sarah did have to do a lot of waiting. But when I get to heaven, if the Lord grants me the opportunity to ask her if it was worth it, I'm pretty sure she will say it was.

After her long wait, God's time for the miracle of Isaac had come. The Lord made a personal appearance to Abraham to tell him the fabulous news:

The Lord appeared to Abraham near the great trees of Mamre while he was sitting at the entrance to his tent in the heat of the day. Abraham looked up and saw three men standing nearby. When he saw them, he hurried from the entrance of his tent to meet them and bowed low to the ground.

He said, "If I have found favor in your eyes, my lord, do not pass your servant by. Let a little water be brought, and then you may all wash your feet and rest under this tree. Let me get you something to eat, so you can be refreshed and then go on your way—now that you have come to your servant."

"Very well," they answered, "do as you say."

So Abraham hurried into the tent to Sarah. "Quick," he said, "get three seahs of fine flour and knead it and bake some bread."

Then he ran to the herd and selected a choice, tender calf and gave it to a servant, who hurried to prepare it. He then brought some curds and milk and the calf that had been prepared, and set these before them. While they ate, he stood near them under a tree.

"Where is your wife Sarah?" they asked him.

"There, in the tent," he said.

Then the Lord said, "I will surely return to you about this time next year, and Sarah your wife will have a son."

Now Sarah was listening at the entrance to the tent, which was behind him. Abraham and Sarah were already old and well advanced in years, and Sarah was past the age of childbearing. So Sarah laughed to herself as she thought, "After I am worn out and my master is old, will I now have this pleasure?"

Then the Lord said to Abraham, "Why did Sarah laugh and say, 'Will I really have a child, now that I am old?' Is anything too hard for the Lord? I will return to you at the appointed time next year and Sarah will have a son."

Sarah was afraid, so she lied and said, "I did not laugh."

But he said, "Yes, you did laugh" (Genesis 18:1-15).

The time was near. God's promise was going to be fulfilled. The promise, however, was against all odds, all logic, and all reality. For Abraham and Sarah, having a child at this time in their lives had seemed hopeless.

Sarah heard the conversation going on between the Lord (in the form of a man) and Abraham. When she heard that she would have a son the next year, she laughed to herself. Come on! For all intents and purposes, her womb was as good as dead. Even though the Bible says she *laughed to herself*, the Lord heard her. Oops! He caught her.

Why do we think we can hide a thought or deny a feeling from our Lord? Look what David says in Psalm 139:1-10:

O Lord, you have searched me and you know me. You know when I sit and when I rise; you perceive my thoughts from afar. You discern my going out and my lying down; you are familiar with all my ways. Before a word is on my tongue you know it completely, O Lord.

You hem me in—behind and before; you have laid your hand upon me. Such knowledge is too wonderful for me, too lofty for me to attain.

Where can I go from your Spirit? Where can I flee from your presence? If I go up to the heavens, you are there; if I make my bed in the depths, you are there. If I rise on the wings of the dawn, if I settle on the far side of the sea, even there your hand will guide me, your right hand will hold me fast.

That is clear. We hide nothing; He knows everything. I suppose that is why David ends this beautiful Psalm the way he does:

Search me, O God, and know my heart; test me and know my anxious thoughts. See if there is any offensive way in me, and lead me in the way everlasting (Psalm 139:23-24).

The Lord loved Sarah and wanted to teach her that nothing is ever hidden from Him, so He confronted her about her lie. That was not comfortable. We, like Sarah, might also get defensive and lie, but who are we kidding? He knows our heart—He knows our thoughts.

The Lord asked Sarah a very important question in Genesis 18:14. He made her take a really good look at what she believed about the God she served. *"Is anything too hard for the Lord?"*

It is easy to say, "Oh no, nothing is too hard for the Lord," but when our lives are involved, it's not always so easy to act on that fact.

That is a powerful question for all of us. I found a few stories of Jesus in the gospels as proof that nothing is impossible for Him.

In Mark 10:17-27:

> *As Jesus started on his way, a man ran up to him and fell on his knees before him. "Good teacher," he asked, "what must I do to inherit eternal life?"*
>
> *"Why do you call me good?" Jesus answered. "No one is good—except God alone. You know the commandments: 'Do not murder, do not commit adultery, do not steal, do not give false testimony, do not defraud, honor your father and mother.'"*
>
> *"Teacher," he declared, "all these I have kept since I was a boy."*
>
> *Jesus looked at him and loved him. "One thing you lack," he said. "Go, sell everything you have and give to the poor,*

*and you will have treasure in heaven. Then
come, follow me."*

*At this the man's face fell. He went
away sad, because he had great wealth.*

*Jesus looked around and said to his
disciples, "How hard it is for the rich to
enter the kingdom of God!"*

*The disciples were amazed at his
words. But Jesus said again, "Children,
how hard it is to enter the kingdom of God!
It is easier for a camel to go through the
eye of a needle than for a rich man to enter
the kingdom of God."*

*The disciples were even more
amazed, and said to each other, "Who then
can be saved?"*

*Jesus looked at them and said, "With
man this is impossible, but not with God;
all things are possible with God."*

In this story of the rich young man, the disciples
looked at everything this man had: youth, money,
prestige, and power. He had also kept all the
commandments. They thought that if he couldn't get in,
no one could. God saves by grace, by faith in Jesus, and
by a surrendered life—not by works. He saves us on His
terms, and nothing, I mean nothing is too hard for Him.

And from John 3:1-18:

Now there was a man of the Pharisees named Nicodemus, a member of the Jewish ruling council. He came to Jesus at night and said, "Rabbi, we know you are a teacher who has come from God. For no one could perform the miraculous signs you are doing if God were not with him."

In reply Jesus declared, "I tell you the truth, no one can see the kingdom of God unless he is born again."

"How can a man be born when he is old?" Nicodemus asked. "Surely he cannot enter a second time into his mother's womb to be born!"

Jesus answered, "I tell you the truth, no one can enter the kingdom of God unless he is born of water and the Spirit. Flesh gives birth to flesh, but the Spirit gives birth to spirit. You should not be surprised at my saying, 'You must be born again.' The wind blows wherever it pleases. You hear its sound, but you cannot tell where it comes from or where it is going. So it is with everyone born of the Spirit."

"How can this be?" Nicodemus asked.

"You are Israel's teacher," said Jesus, "and do you not understand these things? I tell you the truth, we speak of what we know, and we testify to what we have seen, but still .you people do not

accept our testimony. I have spoken to you of earthly things and you do not believe; how then will you believe if I speak of heavenly things? No one has ever gone into heaven except the one who came from heaven—the Son of Man. Just as Moses lifted up the snake in the desert, so the Son of Man must be lifted up, that everyone who believes in him may have eternal life.

"For God so loved the world that he gave his one and only Son, that whoever believes in him shall not perish but have eternal life. For God did not send his Son into the world to condemn the world, but to save the world through him. Whoever believes in him is not condemned, but whoever does not believe stands condemned already because he has not believed in the name of God's one and only Son."

Jesus made it possible for you and me to be born again. For God so loved Lynnelle Pierce that He gave her Jesus. If she would just believe with all her heart in Him as her Savior and Lord, she would not perish, but have eternal life. I see that miracle continuing as I walk with Him on my spiritual journey. I have been reborn, and I see a new life emerge as Lynnelle becomes less and less and Jesus becomes more and more in me. So, believe me, I know that nothing, I repeat nothing, is too hard for the Lord.

Hanging near my back door is a plaque given to me by a dear friend. This plaque has that very question on it—*"Is anything too hard for the Lord?"* It is the first thing I see when I walk into my home, and it is the last thing I see when I leave. Whatever situation I find myself in—at home or away—I am constantly being reminded that nothing is too hard for my Lord, and He wants me always turning to Him.

When I read this story of Abraham and Sarah and look with only human understanding at the hopeless reality of the situation, I remember that God did promise, and I'm directed to the meaning of faith in Hebrews 11:1:

Now faith is being sure of what we hope for and certain of what we do not see.

Our situation may seem hopeless, but our hope is not in the situation anyway. It is in Jesus, the promised Messiah. He and all of His promises are our only hope.

Though Abraham had some shaky moments, in his heart he demonstrated faith in God in spite of a seemingly hopeless situation.

"Abraham believed God, and it was credited to him as righteousness" (Romans 4:3b).

Paul goes on to tell us later in this same chapter,

Against all hope, Abraham in hope believed and so became the father of many nations, just as it had been said to him, "So shall your offspring be." Without weakening in his faith, he faced the fact that his body was as good as dead—since he was about a hundred years old—and that Sarah's womb was also dead. Yet he did not waver through unbelief regarding the promise of God, but was strengthened in his faith and gave glory to God, being fully persuaded that God had power to do what he had promised (Romans 4:18-21).

I just love it! I refer to those verses so often when I get shaky knees. Wouldn't it be absolutely wonderful to have someone look at our hopeless situation, watch us react, and then be able to say about us: "She did not waver through unbelief regarding the promise of God. Instead, she was strengthened in her faith and gave glory to God because she was fully persuaded that God had the power to do what He had promised."

No doubt—no debate—no more discussion.

My God is real, and so are His promises. I expect BIG things, because I know and serve a big and awesome God.

3

MIRIAM

When I was a little girl, one of the Bible stories I always loved to hear was the story of Moses. The story, though, didn't start out positively. Life was very difficult for the Israelites. The new Pharaoh was terribly threatened by the increase in the number of Israelites. In order to take care of this problem, he decreed that every Israelite boy who was born must be thrown into the Nile, but girls would be allowed to live. Here is the story from Exodus 2:1-10.

Now a man of the house of Levi married a Levite woman, and she became pregnant and gave birth to a son. When she saw that he was a fine child, she hid him for three months. But when she could hide him no longer, she got a papyrus basket for him and coated it with tar and pitch. Then she placed the child in it and put it among the reeds along the bank of the Nile. His sister stood at a distance to see what would happen to him.

Then Pharaoh's daughter went down to the Nile to bathe, and her attendants were walking along the river bank. She saw the basket among the reeds and sent her slave girl to get it. She opened it and saw the baby. He was crying, and she felt sorry for him. "This is one of the Hebrew babies," she said.

Then his sister asked Pharaoh's daughter, "Shall I go and get one of the Hebrew women to nurse the baby for you?"

"Yes, go," she answered. And the girl went and got the baby's mother. Pharaoh's daughter said to her, "Take this baby and nurse him for me, and I will pay you." So the woman took the baby and nursed him. When the child grew older, she took him to Pharaoh's daughter and he became her son. She named him Moses, saying, "I drew him out of the water."

What a vital part Moses' sister played in the life of Moses. Her name was Miriam. From an early age, she exemplified fine character qualities. She was loving and obedient. After God had chosen Moses to lead the Israelites out of bondage, she continued to help Moses as a support, a prophetess, and a leader.

Then Miriam the prophetess, Aaron's sister, took a tambourine in her hand, and all the women followed her, with

*tambourines and dancing. Miriam sang to
them:*
    *"Sing to the Lord, for he is highly
exalted. The horse and its rider he has
hurled into the sea" (Exodus 15:20-21).*

    *"I brought you up out of Egypt and
redeemed you from the land of slavery. I
sent Moses to lead you, also Aaron and
Miriam" (Micah 6:4).*

Yes, she was wonderful, wasn't she? But we are
also able to use her as an example of a critical spirit.
(That is a whiny, self-centered attitude that deliberately
wants to hurt and put down another to lift up one's self.)
How is that possible? It is the same old broken record
story. She took her eyes off the Lord and saw only
herself. The story goes like this:

    *Miriam and Aaron began to talk
against Moses because of his Cushite wife,
for he had married a Cushite. "Has the
Lord spoken only through Moses?" they
asked. "Hasn't he also spoken through us?"
And the Lord heard this.*
    *(Now Moses was a very humble man,
more humble than anyone else on the face
of the earth.)*
    *At once the Lord said to Moses,
Aaron and Miriam, "Come out to the Tent
of Meeting, all three of you." So the three*

of them came out. Then the Lord came down in a pillar of cloud; he stood at the entrance to the Tent and summoned Aaron and Miriam. When both of them stepped forward, he said, "Listen to my words:

"When a prophet of the Lord is among you, I reveal myself to him in visions, I speak to him in dreams. But this is not true of my servant Moses; he is faithful in all my house. With him I speak face to face, clearly and not in riddles; he sees the form of the Lord. Why then were you not afraid to speak against my servant Moses?"

The anger of the Lord burned against them, and he left them.

When the cloud lifted from above the Tent, there stood Miriam—leprous, like snow. Aaron turned toward her and saw that she had leprosy; and he said to Moses, "Please, my lord, do not hold against us the sin we have so foolishly committed. Do not let her be like a stillborn infant coming from its mother's womb with its flesh half eaten away."

So Moses cried out to the Lord, "O God, please heal her!"

The Lord replied to Moses, "If her father had spit in her face, would she not have been in disgrace for seven days? Confine her outside the camp for seven

days; after that she can be brought back."
So Miriam was confined outside the camp
for seven days, and the people did not move
on till she was brought back
(Numbers 12:1-15).

Miriam and her other brother Aaron had begun
talking against Moses. They needed an excuse for doing
that, so they had used their sister-in-law and the fact that
the Lord had placed them in a subservient position to
Moses. Yes, the three were a team, but God had called
Moses to be the leader. How quickly they forgot!

Isn't it something how a fight for position can
throw everything out of whack? Moses was the leader,
doing exactly what he was supposed to do—not at all
affected by position. Numbers 12:3 notes that he was *a*
very humble man, more humble than anyone else on the
face of the earth.

Maybe it is important to note here the meaning of
humility. Many times this term gets misconstrued.
Humility is not walking around with your head down
saying, "Oh what a worm I am." The apostle Paul talks
about the meaning of false humility in Colossians 2. That
chapter is proof that there is a humility that is really not
humility. I have always believed that if I have to tell
people how humble I am, I'm probably not very humble.
Humility is a characteristic that is simply there, and it
grows the more I fall in love with Jesus. One cannot
force a humble character. I always look at humility as the
Lord in His right place and me in mine. That always
keeps my Lord above me, and I always have to look up

to see Him. Then, my eyes cannot naturally look at myself or others around me. My eyes are fixed on Him, where they are supposed to be. My total dependence on Him is almost overwhelming. Then, out of the overflow of my life, comes this kind of action:

> *Do nothing out of selfish ambition or vain conceit, but in humility consider others better than yourselves. Each of you should look not only to your own interests, but also to the interests of others (Phil. 2:3-4).*

Jesus is our best example of true humility. Philippians 2 goes on to describe what our attitude should be—the same as that of Christ Jesus,

> *Who, being in very nature God, did not consider equality with God something to be grasped, but made himself nothing, taking the very nature of a servant, being made in human likeness. And being found in appearance as a man, he humbled himself and became obedient to death—even death on a cross! Therefore God exalted him to the highest place and gave him the name that is above every name, that at the name of Jesus every knee should bow, in heaven and on earth and under the earth, and every tongue confess that Jesus Christ is Lord, to the glory of God the Father (V. 6-11).*

The problem was not really about Moses. The problem was within Miriam and Aaron. Moses did not even realize what was going on behind his back, which, by the way, is usually where criticism takes place. You never hear the phrase, "That was a stab in the front." Rather, you hear, "It was a stab in the back." It usually happens when the poor person is not even there to be able to set the story straight.

Well, I finally said the word criticism. The mere word makes my skin crawl. Criticism is very dangerous, and that Old Testament story warns us of that. Let me clarify my position on the use of the word criticism. The dictionary defines criticism in two distinct ways. First, it is used to describe judgments of the merits and faults of books, music, and art rendered by individuals in a given field (art, music, and literature critics). I view this definition of criticism as judgment or evaluation of human works and their comparable value and worth based on current and historical human standards. The second definition of criticism is described as disapproval and fault-finding. The difference is significant, as this use of criticism is judgment or evaluation of a person's worth, value, attitude or point of view—not of works! My use of and description of criticism in this book is based on the disapproval, fault-finding, or judgment of a person. Jesus' instructions are very clear on the subject of judging others:

> *"Do not judge, or you too will be judged.*
> *For in the same way you judge others, you*
> *will be judged, and with the measure you*

use, it will be measured to you"
(Matthew 7:1-2).

Like so many inner strifes, criticism is a "self" problem. Behind a critical spirit is a need for self-elevation, usually accompanied by feelings of jealousy, envy, insecurity, and others, I'm sure.

In Numbers 11:16-17, God had told Moses to bring to Him seventy of Israel's elders who were known as leaders and officials among the people. They would help carry the burden of the people, so that Moses would not have to carry it alone.

Knowing this, Miriam obviously felt her position was being challenged. She might have felt she wasn't needed like she used to be (and that is a horrible feeling, isn't it?)

When our eyes come off the Lord, and we go through what Miriam was going through, it is very understandable that the feelings of jealousy, envy, insecurity, and a need for self-elevation creep in. When we take our eyes off the Lord and focus on "self," we may create an outpouring of criticism which puts someone else down so that we don't look so bad.

Somehow, we "pooh-pooh" the sin of criticism. We think no one will know. We have a tendency to forget that the Lord knows our heart and mind. He hears words before we even say them out loud. And when it comes to criticism, the Bible also says it is the seventh thing that the Lord hates and thinks is detestable—*a man who stirs up dissension among brothers* (Proverbs 6:19b).

The Lord looks at criticism very seriously, and His reaction to Miriam and Aaron proved it. God called a family meeting and included Moses. The Lord wanted Moses in on this. The Bible says the *anger of the Lord burned against them* (Miriam and Aaron), and He left them with Miriam standing there with leprosy. That is taking a critical spirit very seriously!

When I read that the Lord's anger burned, I was reminded of two other places in Scripture where the Lord was angry. I do not like to think of the Lord angry—He's loving. But when the Lord is angry, He's justified in being so. Back in Exodus 3 and 4 when God called Moses to lead the Israelites out of Egypt, Moses kept giving one excuse after another. The Lord was patient, but only up to a point. Finally, in Exodus 4:14, even after all of the Lord's reassuring words, sustaining comfort, and the promises of His very presence, Moses pleaded with the Lord to send someone else, and then the Lord's anger burned.

In Romans 1:18-19, Paul told the Romans that,

> *The wrath of God is being revealed from heaven against all the godlessness and wickedness of men who suppress the truth by their wickedness, since what may be known about God is plain to them, because God has made it plain to them.*

The anger or wrath of God is a terrifying thing, but it is justified, because those who are the recipients of it deserve it. Anger is an emotion, not sinful in and of itself. God's anger and wrath on His people is, believe it or not, bathed in love. He hates sin so badly but loves His people so much that He often uses His anger to bring us back on track. He wants us off the path of sin and back on the track of righteousness, living a life pleasing to Him.

When we experience God's anger on this earth, we are experiencing His love, mercy, and grace. His saving grace will also prevent us from experiencing His final anger and wrath on judgment day, which will keep us out of eternal hell.

So, does God get mad? Does He really get angry? You bet He does—and we can be grateful that He does. I pray you look into your heart and see Jesus there so that you never have to discover what His final anger is all about.

Let's look back at Numbers 12:10-13. There stood Moses and Aaron looking at their sister with the awful disease of leprosy. Even after all Miriam's criticisms of Moses, he still begged God to heal her. Did you notice how family bonds came to the rescue? Many times in family relationships there are few things members have in common other than the family unit itself and the love that the family unit shares. Each family member is a distinct individual with different interests, yet bound together by the strength of the family unit.

For instance, I have two brothers who love me very much and would give their lives for me (and I for them), but, like Miriam and Aaron, I am certain we have hurt each other along the way, too. We have different interests, and our lives have gone in different directions.

Even though the same family blood flows through our veins, we are very different. No, I do not see them every day or even talk to them every day. But, I do have the assurance that one little phone call would bring them to me instantly if I needed them. I have no doubt about that at all. It is one of the greatest, most secure feelings I have.

I remember one time when my brother and I were in grade school together. I was in the third grade, and he was in kindergarten. At home we were typical siblings, but at school, I felt protective of him. Word had reached me that a kid was picking on my brother. So, during recess, I calmly went over to his section of the playground and made sure that brute of a kid knew that my little brother had a BIG sister. I was fearless when it came to my brother's safety. When it comes right down to it, family is tight.

Returning to the story, we see that the family unit of Miriam, Moses, and Aaron was still tight. Aaron turned to Moses and addressed him as "my lord." All of a sudden position was back in its proper place. He begged Moses to do something. Moses cried to the Lord to heal Miriam.

The Lord heard Moses' plea, but shared with Moses that sin has its penalties. Miriam had to learn about true humility. There are always reasons why God does what He does. He is always teaching, because we have so much to learn. That never changes.

I could not help but wonder why Miriam got the harsh punishment and not Aaron. At first, I thought that maybe Miriam instigated the whole ordeal. But then, I thought about the family thing again. When I watch someone I love go through a discipline alone when I know full well I am just as guilty—that is torture in itself. So, could it be that Aaron also experienced discipline, maybe even more difficult than Miriam's?

Even though the problem was only between God, Moses, Aaron, and Miriam, by causing Miriam to be an outcast for seven days, the whole company of people Moses was leading had to wait. Her sin affected them all (just a reminder what sin can do). It showed everyone again that criticism is a sin—and the Lord will not stand for it.

As I was studying this and pondering what criticism really is, I could not help but notice a real distinction between criticism and correcting. Correcting is something we all need, but do we like it? Probably not! Read Proverbs 6:23:

> *For these commands are a lamp, this teaching is a light, and the corrections of discipline are the way to life.*

Correcting is a must. That's just the way it is. So what makes that different from criticism? A lot! The root reason for correction is LOVE. We want the best for the person we are correcting. We have his or her best interest in mind. We have a deep desire to correct a wrong, because we know that sin always takes us on a downward spiral if we do not deal with it. In other words, the person we love is only going to get worse, and it's up to us to do something about it.

I have four people in my life to whom I have given the authority to watch me like a hawk. I carefully chose these specific people because I know that they love me and want me at my best. If by any chance I veer off course in my teaching or singing, they have the right to pounce. I wish I could tell you that they have never had to approach me. But I can't. Throughout the years of my ministry, if my eyes have gotten off the Lord for one second, it makes a difference, it's obvious, and they have called me on it. Most of the time, I hadn't even realized it yet. Now, in all honesty, have I enjoyed their correction? Absolutely not! The natural response is to go on the defensive, put on the boxing gloves, and duke it out. Excuses, excuses. But they love me. I know it. They're right. I listen and obey. I'm back on track. Thank You, Lord.

> *No discipline seems pleasant at the time,*
> *but painful. Later on, however, it produces*
> *a harvest of righteousness and peace for*
> *those who have been trained by it*
> *(Hebrews 12:11).*

Now criticism is another matter. Criticism is not bathed in love. In fact, just the opposite. I'll go as far as to say criticism is of the devil, because it cuts down, creates doubt, and eventually can lead to destruction. Didn't we learn about doubt and destruction from our lesson on Eve?

Being a public personality, I get my share of criticism, most of it behind my back, but every once in a while, to my face. The ones criticizing the loudest are the people who have never really met me but think they know me. Trust me, I have learned the difference between correction and criticism, and the experience hasn't been pleasant.

One lesson, for example, was at a little church out in the middle of nowhere. As I was singing to this group of people, I noticed a woman in the audience with the most unappealing look on her face. It was not sad, but sour. She was miserable, and it showed.

After the concert, she sat me down to tell me that she thought I was a disgrace to the name of Jesus. Needless to say, I was shocked, hurt, and crushed. These were just a few of the emotions that began to stir in me because of her cruel statement. Let me tell you, I had never met this woman before in my life. The concert itself went wonderfully. In fact, a man was saved that night. There was no doubt that the Lord had His hand of blessing on the concert as a whole. This woman's intent was to tear me down.

She went on to give me a list of reasons why she had this strong opinion. I prayed, the Lord took over my natural feelings of defensiveness, and He helped me to just listen. When she finished with an attitude of "there—take that," I couldn't believe how my attitude had changed from when she first started in on me with all of her guns loaded. My anger and "how dare you" attitude changed into sympathy. She had totally missed the joy of the Lord. Apparently she was miserable, and she wanted me miserable too. Believe me, there was no justification for her statement. She did not know me. She didn't love me or have my best interest in mind. Did I lash back? No, I did not. I couldn't believe how calm I was. I know the Lord was with me every step of the way. I told her that I would consider all she had said, but when doing that, I would weigh it against all the other comments I had received. I told her that no one had ever before said to me that I was a disgrace to Jesus' name. She got up in a huff and left. Still not quite believing that had all happened, I sat there for a minute. I had asked the Lord to give me the words; now I was reflecting on what I know to be true. I know that Jesus lives in me, and what lives in me should be reflecting out of my face. So, my prayer is that people see Jesus, and that is exactly the way it should be. That would prove I am not a disgrace to Jesus' name. Settled. Case closed.

I am just so sorry that whole episode happened. I can receive a hundred encouraging comments, but just one negative one can wear me down to a pulp even when I know it's uncalled for. See my point? Criticism tears down. It is dangerous. Remember, earlier I said criticism is of the devil, so it must be a tool of destruction.

I've been back to that little church, but she is no longer a member there. I pray that she is no longer miserable, but instead has made the choice to receive the joy of the Lord in her life. As for me, with the Lord I move on, and I will not let the devil, through criticism, plant that seed of doubt. Get behind me, Satan!

Criticism can do more than just hurt and crush feelings. The danger comes when it starts tearing down a reputation—even killing a ministry.

Years ago I had a large concert to give for a combination of churches that were getting together. I was really looking forward to it. Two weeks before the engagement, I received a call from the hosting pastor. He said he was sorry to call, but a man in his church had told him that I had a drinking problem. Because of that, sinners like me were not even allowed in his church, let alone permitted to perform in it. I thought he was kidding me, but he assured me he was dead serious. I couldn't believe it. For one thing, aren't churches supposed to be a hospital for the sick and needy rather than a country club for the saints? Even if I had that problem, his attitude was wrong. But the whole thing was a cruel, calculated lie. I not only don't have a drinking problem, I never drink. I never have. The man who started that awful rumor was a struggling singer, who apparently thought that if he could get me out of the picture, he would sing for this gathering. Seeing that he did not have any "dirty" laundry on me, he decided to make some up—and it worked. I lost the singing engagement, and he got it.

I was devastated to say the least. I was certain that a story like that would ruin our ministry. I remember hanging up the phone, crying, and falling to my knees. I could not imagine anyone doing this to me. Our situation looked mighty bleak, but my husband Tom and I decided not to fight back. We handed it over completely to the Lord. He knew our hearts and saw our actions, so of course, He knew the truth. Romans 12:17-21 came to our minds, and we chose to obey God's words:

Do not repay anyone evil for evil. Be careful to do what is right in the eyes of everybody. If it is possible, as far as it depends on you, live at peace with everyone. Do not take revenge, my friends, but leave room for God's wrath, for it is written: "It is mine to avenge; I will repay," says the Lord. On the contrary:
"If your enemy is hungry, feed him; if he is thirsty, give him something to drink. In doing this, you will heap burning coals on his head."
Do not be overcome by evil, but overcome evil with good.

God has a way of working it all out. Years later our ministry is stronger than ever. In fact, the minister who had a part in it all called to apologize and admit the committee's mistake.

Criticism, however, is dangerous. It can have lasting and deadly results. Its consequences affect many.

Our world and our churches would be dramatically changed if everyone knew the difference between correction and criticism and lived by these verses:

Therefore encourage one another and build each other up, just as in fact you are doing (I Thessalonians 5:11).

Brothers, if someone is caught in a sin, you who are spiritual should restore him gently.

*But watch yourself, or you also may be
tempted. Carry each other's burdens, and
in this way you will fulfill the law of Christ
(Galatians 6:1-2).*

*Therefore, as God's chosen people, holy
and dearly loved, clothe yourselves with
compassion, kindness, humility, gentleness
and patience. Bear with each other and
forgive whatever grievances you may have
against one another. Forgive as the Lord
forgave you. And over all these virtues put
on love, which binds them all together in
perfect unity (Colossians 3:12-14).*

Thank You, Lord, for saying it so perfectly. There is no
doubt in my mind that Miriam was a wonderful, godly,
and gifted woman. The Lord had definite plans for her,
and when she followed those plans, her godly character
came out in full force. But, we learned a valuable, visible
lesson when we saw her lose track of God's plan and
solely concentrate on her own plan, which led to ugly
vindictiveness and very stern consequences. It was not a
pretty sight. She learned, and now we learn from her that
God's ways are the best ways. Let's leave it at that!

4

RAHAB

In order to get an appreciation of the character of this Old Testament woman, we must understand the circumstances that existed in her time. Moses had died, and his successor, Joshua, was now ready to lead the Israelites into the land that God had promised. Sure, that sounds easy—no problem, right? Wrong—the land was swarming with enemies. Yes, the promised land was smack-dab in enemy territory. Follow this exciting story from Joshua 2.

Then Joshua son of Nun secretly sent two spies from Shittim. "Go, look over the land," he said, "especially Jericho." So they went and entered the house of a prostitute named Rahab and stayed there.
The king of Jericho was told, "Look! Some of the Israelites have come here tonight to spy out the land." So the king of Jericho sent this message to Rahab: "Bring out the men who came to you and entered your house, because they have come to spy out the whole land."

But the woman had taken the two men and hidden them. She said, "Yes, the men came to me, but I did not know where they had come from. At dusk, when it was time to close the city gate, the men left. I don't know which way they went. Go after them quickly. You may catch up with them." (But she had taken them up to the roof and hidden them under the stalks of flax she had laid out on the roof.) So the men set out in pursuit of the spies on the road that leads to the fords of the Jordan, and as soon as the pursuers had gone out, the gate was shut.

Before the spies lay down for the night, she went up on the roof and said to them, "I know that the Lord has given this land to you and that a great fear of you has fallen on us, so that all who live in this country are melting in fear because of you. We have heard how the Lord dried up the water of the Red Sea for you when you came out of Egypt, and what you did to Sihon and Og, the two kings of the Amorites east of the Jordan, whom you completely destroyed. When we heard of it, our hearts melted and everyone's courage failed because of you, for the Lord your God is God in heaven above and on the earth below. Now then, please swear to me by the Lord that you will show kindness to my family, because I have shown kindness to you. Give me a sure sign that you will spare the lives of my father and mother, my brothers and sisters, and all who belong to them, and that you will save us from death."

"Our lives for your lives!" the men assured her. "If you don't tell what we are doing, we will treat you kindly and faithfully when the Lord gives us the land."

So she let them down by a rope through the window, for the house she lived in was part of the city wall. Now she had said to them, "Go to the hills so the pursuers will not find you. Hide yourselves there three days until they return, and then go on your way."

The men said to her, "This oath you made us swear will not be binding on us unless, when we enter the land, you have tied this scarlet cord in the window through which you let us down, and unless you have brought your father and mother, your brothers and all your family into your house. If anyone goes outside your house into the street, his blood will be on his own head; we will not be responsible. As for anyone who is in the house with you, his blood will be on our head if a hand is laid on him. But if you tell what we are doing, we will be released from the oath you made us swear."

"Agreed," she replied. "Let it be as you say." So she sent them away and they departed. And she tied the scarlet cord in the window.

When they left, they went into the hills and stayed there three days, until the pursuers had searched all along the road and returned without finding them. Then the two men started back. They went down out of the hills, forded the river and came to Joshua son of Nun and told him everything that had happened to them. They said to Joshua, "The Lord has surely given the whole land into our hands; all the people are melting in fear because of us."

Joshua was a strong and courageous man of God with a good head on his shoulders. He secretly sent out two spies to look over the land. Where did the spies decide to set up their look-out point? They chose the house of Rahab, a prostitute.

We don't know very much about her except for that "colorful" fact. So why in the world would they set up there of all places? Wouldn't it be a bit dangerous and also very wrong for men of God to be identified with all of the "activities" that took place at the house of Rahab? Normally, yes, but the choice of this location was actually a wise move. The spies would be quite inconspicuous in this setting. To any suspicious eyes, they would naturally blend in with the many actual male patrons that frequented Rahab's house throughout the day and night. In addition, "Rahab's house was in an ideal location for a quick escape because it was built into the city wall." Also, "God directed the spies to Rahab's house because He knew her heart was open to Him and that she would be instrumental in the Israelite victory over Jericho."[3]

When word reached the king that there were spies in the land, he immediately sent a message to Rahab. But by this time she had already hidden them. Then out of her mouth came the slickest, smoothest lie I have heard in a long time (telling the king's men that the spies had already left). Lying came easy to her. She was good at it and very convincing. Here was a "gutsy" lady who knew how to handle men. She definitely was not easily intimidated.

When I first read that bold lie, I thought, "Why would the Lord use a sin to accomplish His purpose?" I actually asked Him for an answer, because that can cause confusion. After I read the whole story through Joshua 6, I believe He showed me the answer. The Lord will not condone lying for one second. But think about it. She didn't know any better. She had not yet started down the road of sanctification. She was almost ready to confess that the Lord God is God in heaven above and on the earth below. She only knew one lifestyle, that of a shrewd business woman, but sadly, one without Almighty God. She had learned that if it takes lying, lie. It came quite naturally for her. Like any bad habit, the more we do it, the easier it gets.

I repeat—God never condones a sin, but isn't it a relief to know that He'll look past our sin of ignorance and see our heart? That beautiful mustard seed of faith was about to take root, and God loved her. Her motive was pure. I'm certain that as she lived in the house of Israel after all this happened (Joshua 6:25), she learned the lifestyle of a godly woman day-by-day and step-by-step as we all do. If God showed us all at once everything that had to be changed in our lives, we would be defeated before we even took the first step down the sanctification road.

Verses 8-11 were life-changing verses for Rahab. She had an ear that was trained to listen for all types of information. Her house was along the city wall—the center of activity, and with all the men that frequented there, she heard plenty. She did not miss much, and before the spies went to sleep for the night, she wanted to have an all-important chat about what she had heard and had chosen to believe. Because of her faith, she risked her own life by hiding the spies.

Faith comes when we know who our God is, and faith causes us to be selfless.

Hear Paul's words to Timothy in II Timothy 1:12:

That is why I am suffering as I am. Yet I am not ashamed, because I know whom I have believed, and am convinced that he is able to guard what I have entrusted to him for that day.

And I restate the definition of faith from Hebrews 11:1:

*Now faith is being sure of what we hope for
and certain of what we do not see.*

Did you catch the life-changing faith words: convinced, sure, and certain?

Faith has a cumulative effect. The more we get to know God, the more we dare to step out in faith, and it is faith that pleases God.

And without faith it is impossible to please God, because anyone who comes to him must believe that he exists and that he rewards those who earnestly seek him (Hebrews 11:6).

In Joshua 2:9 Rahab said, *"I know,"* which was a statement, not a question. It was not a "maybe" or an "I think," but an *"I know."* That was faith; even her mustard seed of faith pleased God, and He rewarded her for her earnest desire to seek Him by sparing her and her family's lives.

It is said everyone has two sides. That is probably true—a self-trusting side and a God-trusting side. As "colorful" as Rahab's self-trusting side was, we can see her other side starting to evolve—the one touched by God. It is profoundly true that once we have received a touch from God, we are never the same.

Rahab's natural business tactics came alive again, and she started to barter with an "I'll do for you and you do for me" philosophy. At the same time, however, her selfless attitude was very evident. She had a deep concern for her father, mother, brothers, sisters, and all who belonged to them, because she knew that Jericho was going to fall into the hands of God's people.

The oath was made: the spies' lives for her family's lives. But the spies made her step out in faith. No one knew exactly how or when this was all going to transpire, but they still promised her that her family would be safe. The conditions, however, were that her whole family had to be in her house, and a scarlet rope had to be hung in the window from which the spies had escaped.

We read that she agreed and obeyed. Obedience is a very important ingredient in the recipe of faith. Then she waited.

I cannot help but see the significance in the scarlet rope. I believe that was no coincidence. It was the color of blood. The scarlet rope physically saved Rahab and her family, and Jesus' scarlet blood saves all who believe and put their faith and trust in Him.

In Joshua 6, God's plan was carried out. For six days, Joshua, armed men, guards, and priests with trumpets blaring marched around the city once. On the seventh day, they marched around the city seven times, and as they gave a loud shout, the walls of the city collapsed. Only Rahab and all the people in her house were spared.

Rahab moved in faith, and the Lord did what He had promised. But then He always does—in His time.

The Lord is not slow in keeping his promise, as some understand slowness. He

*is patient with you, not wanting anyone to
perish, but everyone to come to repentance
(II Peter 3:9).*

The faith of Rahab was remembered for years to come. "God often uses people with simple faith to accomplish His great purposes, no matter what kind of past they have had or how insignificant they seem to be. Rahab didn't allow her past to keep her from the new role God had for her."[3] The writer of Hebrews listed her in the Hall of Faith in Hebrews 11:31, and in James 2:25, Rahab was declared righteous because of her faith. Imagine that: a prostitute declared righteous—only by the grace of God!

We cannot help but be moved, awed, and humbled by grace. It is so beyond us. It is incomprehensible. That is why, for some, it is so difficult to accept. They are thrilled to be forgiven and to have the burden of their sin lifted. But they still have a hard time looking in the mirror and actually seeing themselves as God sees them—pure and whiter than snow because they have been washed in the blood of the Lamb. For some, the past has a way of rearing it's ugly head, overshadowing God's grace.

In Bible study, I met a precious young woman with that very problem. She admitted to having "quite a past," but praise God, she had experienced His salvation. She also admitted she could not face herself in her mirror every morning. For a long time after her conversion, she could not totally accept His grace.

After one of the Bible studies from the book of
Romans, she came up and shared with me that the Holy
Spirit had very clearly guided her to that special
acceptance of His grace. I couldn't help but ask what she
saw in her mirror now. Her answer was so touching. She
said, "I love my smile." She had never noticed what a
beautiful smile she had—especially one that is fashioned
by the grace of God. It is hard to imagine and understand
that all of our sins and all of our past are forgiven, gone
forevermore.

If we do not accept that gift of grace, we fall into
the trap that allows our past to drag us down. That keeps
us from experiencing Jesus' full forgiveness, His work on
the cross, and His resurrection, which made that
forgiveness possible. What a nasty trap that is! Before we
know it, our past is our excuse for not accepting the free
gift of salvation and a Spirit-filled life. Our past, like
having an albatross around our neck, can weigh us down.
Every one of us has a past. But that is exactly what it
is—past. The Lord has fabulous advice for every believer
with a "past":

> *"Forget the former things; do not dwell on
> the past" (Isaiah 43:18).*

Instead of dwelling on the past, which we can do nothing
about, dwell on Him. Through it all He's been there
supplying us with all our needs for both now and
eternity. Just look at all He's done. Read
Psalm 103:1-14.

> *Praise the Lord, O my soul; all my
> inmost being, praise his holy name. Praise
> the Lord, O my soul, and forget not all his
> benefits—who forgives all your sins and
> heals all your diseases, who redeems your
> life from the pit and crowns you with love
> and compassion, who satisfies your desires
> with good things so that your youth is
> renewed like the eagle's.*
>
> *The Lord works righteousness and
> justice for all the oppressed.*
>
> *He made known his ways to Moses,
> his deeds to the people of Israel: The Lord
> is compassionate and gracious, slow to
> anger, abounding in love. He will not
> always accuse, nor will he harbor his anger
> forever; he does not treat us as our sins
> deserve or repay us according to our
> iniquities. For as high as the heavens are
> above the earth, so great is his love for
> those who fear him; as far as the east is
> from the west, so far has he removed our
> transgressions from us. As a father has
> compassion on his children, so the Lord has
> compassion on those who fear him; for he
> knows how we are formed, he remembers
> that we are dust.*

Let it go! Feel the freedom. Move forward *toward
the goal to win the prize for which God has called me
heavenward in Christ Jesus* (Philippians 3:14).

If we choose to open our eyes, we will see that God has reasons for the hard times we experienced in our past. In II Corinthians 1, we learn that difficulties teach us to rely on God and not ourselves. He also shows us that our past can be used to help others. Don't we find that taking advice or counsel from someone who has walked in our shoes carries a lot more credibility than taking it from someone who is simply trying to give us just "words"? God knows how even our past can be used to further His kingdom if directed the right way—His way.

The apostle Paul was another example of someone with a terrible past, and he knew it.

"Lord," Ananias answered, "I have heard many reports about this man and all the harm he has done to your saints in Jerusalem" (Acts 9:13).

"Many a time I went from one synagogue to another to have them punished, and I tried to force them to blaspheme. In my obsession against them, I even went to foreign cities to persecute them" (Acts 26:11).

I thank Christ Jesus our Lord, who has given me strength, that he considered me faithful, appointing me to his service. Even though I was once a blasphemer and a persecutor and a violent man, I was shown mercy because I acted in ignorance and unbelief. The grace of our Lord was poured out on me abundantly, along with the faith and love that are in Christ Jesus.

Here is a trustworthy saying that deserves full acceptance: Christ Jesus came into the world to save sinners—of whom I am the worst. But for that very reason I was shown mercy so that in me, the worst of sinners, Christ Jesus might display his unlimited patience as an example for those who would believe on him and receive eternal life. Now to the King eternal, immortal, invisible, the only God, be honor and glory for ever and ever. Amen (I Timothy 1:12-17).

Aren't those words the greatest? Can't you just hear the relief and joy in his words for a past forgiven?

He dealt with his past. He never forgot it, but he moved on, and I am thankful he did. I cannot imagine the Bible without Paul's letters.

If you are still not convinced to bag your past baggage, consider this verse from Hebrews 9:14.

How much more, then, will the blood of Christ, who through the eternal Spirit offered himself unblemished to God, cleanse our consciences from acts that lead to death, so that we may serve the living God!

I have a dear friend who did just that. Briefly, let me tell you her "Rahab-type" past. She did not know the Lord, and her marriage was failing. She and her husband went their separate ways. Her way led to drinking, drugs, and prostitution. God's grace, however, brought her and her husband to a seminar. There, they heard about the forgiving power of Jesus; they accepted that grace and were saved—from themselves, their sin, their past, and eternal hell. Their marriage was mended, and together they now have a ministry to inner-city children. They house them, clothe them, feed them, and love them through Jesus. The children are taught to memorize whole chapters of Scripture at one time and to sing songs about Jesus from the bottom of their hearts.

Perhaps you or I could not minister in the trenches of the dangerous inner-city. We might be scared to death. But she's been there and experienced life on the streets. She's been around those blocks quite a few times and is absolutely unafraid. She believes that the Lord has called her back into familiar territory—now her mission field—to serve her living God.

The story of my friend reminds me of a passage of Scripture that frequently gets passed over—Matthew 1. This chapter gives us the lineage of Jesus, and unless we are real family tree buffs, it is usually avoided because of a lack of interest. If you've never studied that chapter, notice now that five women are named in the lineage of Jesus. Out of those five women, four had quite a "colorful" past. Tamar and Rahab were in the prostitution business. Bathsheba was David's mistress, and Ruth (whom we will cover in the next chapter) was a pagan Moabite.

If that is not proof enough that God will take sinners, forgive them, forget their past and then use them—just like he used those women named in Matthew to bring His beloved Son into the world—I don't know what would be!

Yes, God can use our forgiven past and move us forward for His kingdom's sake.

I'm sure you have said this; I know that I have: "Oh, I wish I could go back and redo...." "I wish I knew then what I know now...." "I wish I hadn't wasted all those years...." Don't get discouraged. There is hope. In Joel 2:25, the Lord says, *"I will repay you for the years the locusts have eaten...."*

In other words, God has the ability to fill our lives with blessings. Then our lives in Him become so fruitful; it's as though those wasted years never existed. What a relief!

Grace is so wonderful. We see from this lesson that grace pardons our past, gives us life—today—abundant and with purpose. It secures our future, no matter what happens to us in this world.

So, if you have felt defeated because you think your life is too far gone, think again. It is never too late to turn it all around. He can't wait to pardon your past and *repay you for the years the locusts have eaten.* He is waiting to use you for His glory. Don't waste any more time.

*"...and the one who trusts in him will never
be put to shame" (Romans 9:33b).*

What a promise!

Rahab, you are my kind of gal and definitely one of God's. Thanks for the lesson on faith. What a testimony you will continue to be for years to come, or at least until the Lord returns, and then I can talk to you face to face. What a treat that will be!

5

RUTH
AND
NAOMI

Everyone loves a love story. Men might not admit it, but down deep most men have been smitten by the love bug and have a sense of romance. Now you need to understand that this comment is coming from the all-time romantic. So maybe it is simply wishful thinking on my part, but I do know that love is powerful. I have never met anyone who doesn't need a sincere dose of it.

Love is the first fruit of God's Spirit. It is the essential ingredient of the other eight. Joy, peace, patience, kindness, goodness, faithfulness, gentleness, and self-control all stem from love. Love that is produced by the Holy Spirit is not only real, but everlasting and unconditional. Love that is conjured up by the fruit of self is temporary and conditional.

Our study of Ruth will reveal God's real, everlasting, and unconditional love.

The book of Ruth is so beautiful and almost unbelievable. It reads like a fairy tale, but we know it is absolutely true. It demonstrates God's master plan in action. When one reads the four chapters in that book, he or she can't help but look back and see that only an

Almighty God could have orchestrated a plan so full of extraordinary details.

There was a famine in Bethlehem. Elimelech took his wife, Naomi, and their two sons to the country of Moab. The one son married Orpah and the other married Ruth.

After they had lived there ten years, Elimelech and his sons died, leaving Naomi, Orpah, and Ruth widows. What a severe loss for these three women. Without her husband and sons, Naomi was at an all-time low point in her life. Then, when she heard that the Lord had come to the aid of His people and provided food, she decided it was time to go home to Bethlehem.

Before she started on her way, she turned to her daughters-in-law and gave them their freedom, so to speak, to go back to their mothers' homes and possibly marry again. They were no longer bound to the Jewish laws for remarriage.

There must have been great mutual love and respect for each other in that family. Despite living among a pagan nation and though coming from completely different religious and cultural backgrounds, there had developed a bond that tied these six people together very tightly. The strongest cord that binds families together is the love of the Lord.

Naomi gave her parting words, and then they all wept aloud and kissed each other goodbye. Orpah, being practical, turned and left, but Ruth clung to Naomi. Naomi tried to convince her to follow her sister-in-law. Ruth refused, and her words became Scripture:

But Ruth replied, "Don't urge me to leave you or to turn back from you. Where you go I will go, and where you stay I will stay. Your people will be my people and your God my God. Where you die I will die, and there I will be buried. May the Lord deal with me, be it ever so severely, if anything but death separates you and me" (Ruth 1:16-17).

Naomi realized that Ruth was determined to go with her, so she stopped urging her to follow Orpah.

What extreme loyalty—a loyalty based on selfless, unconditional love directly produced by God within her heart. That heart condition outweighed what her mind told her was practical. She was sacrificing the chance to remarry, to have children, and to begin a whole new life. And for whom? Her mother-in-law! She was stepping into an unknown future, and willing to do it without her family, familiar surroundings, and all the security that would provide for her.

One can't help but ask, "Who motivated such loyalty?" There is only one explanation: the Lord. Somehow, sometime during those ten years, Ruth changed from worshiping pagan gods to loving the one true God. When God changes a heart, everything changes—especially the attitude and purpose for living. So when Naomi's God became Ruth's God, Ruth began a relationship that changed her entire life.

When our hearts are turned toward the Lord, our ears are, too. We hear His call. Ruth heard God's call.

Now, she did not know at that time that she would
become the great grandmother of David, who continued
the line from which Jesus came. Ruth only knew she had
heard the call of God, and she moved in obedience to His
will.

Two major questions Christians ask today are,
"How can we determine or know God's will for our
lives?" "He doesn't speak to us in an audible voice, so do
we have to just guess at what He wants?" Those are
important questions. How can we obey God if the
answers are hazy or if we're simply trusting our feelings,
which can be fickle and out of control? There is a way
we can know. First, fall on our knees with our Bibles
open and read this verse:

> *I keep asking that the God of our Lord*
> *Jesus Christ, the glorious Father, may give*
> *you the Spirit of wisdom and revelation, so*
> *that you may know him better*
> *(Ephesians 1:17).*

God answers prayer. Remember, Jesus said,

> *"Ask and it will be given to you; seek and*
> *you will find; knock and the door will be*
> *opened to you" (Matthew 7:7).*

God's Word has something to say that will always
relate to your issues at hand. Search for it; find it. The
Lord will never ask you to do anything that is wrong or

that contradicts His very Word. His Word gives answers for our lives.

Secondly, seek advice from a spiritual leader who is mature in the Lord and trustworthy in his or her faith. This person will not just tell you what you want to hear, but will steady you on or steer you onto God's path.

Thirdly, look for confirming circumstances. Watch for doors to open or close. Make certain that this step is third, not first. The story of Jonah proves that. There just so happened to be a ship going to Tarshish—how convenient, but it was not the will of God for Jonah to travel to Tarshish. The will of God was for him to go to Ninevah, and God did get Jonah there, didn't He? God's will, let there be no doubt, will be accomplished.

Fourthly, wait and listen for God's answer. Don't be impulsive. So often we miss God's best for us when we don't wait. Remember, God is on His own timetable.

Lastly, experience His peace. I can't explain that one. You'll just have to experience it for yourself. But believe me, you'll know it when you have it.

The Lord calls all of us to different tasks and different jobs. We can't all be foreign missionaries. He needs to position His people in all walks of life. So wherever He positions us, He expects us to go into our world and share the Gospel, the best news of Jesus, the Light of the world. With Him living in our hearts, our faces should be shining brightly, radiating the light of Jesus. Wherever God's will places us, always know that God's will is good, pleasing, and perfect (Romans 12:2).

It is such a comfort to know that we will not miss God's will for us. When we seek Him, we will find Him (Proverbs 8:17 and Luke 11:9).

I remember when God called Tom and me into full-time ministry. We bucked the call for awhile, not wanting to leave a steady job and the security of a weekly salary. But, when God calls, He means it. He is a God of unity. So His call was the same to Tom and me. He called us to be a team for His kingdom, to surrender all that was practical and just trust Him.

It's been many years now, and I would not trade all the experiences and spiritual growth it has provided for any other job in the world.

What is so precious is that not only did God call Tom and me, He called our children too. So often I've been asked how our children have handled the ministry. It caused our boys to find out that Jesus is real and that He changes lives. That's worth everything to me.

When our son Jason was five, we were scheduled to do a concert about an hour's drive from home. That afternoon Jason came down with the flu. I called my mom, and she willingly consented to take care of him and our other son Chad that evening. As the hour drew near to leave, I looked at my sick little sweetheart, and I couldn't go. I just couldn't leave that little boy. He heard me tell Tom to call the people and apologize, but we had a sick child, and he had to come first.

I heard, "Mom, Mom, you have to go. Maybe there is one person there that needs to hear you tell them about Jesus. I'll be O.K. Nana's coming." Tears rolled down my face as I realized that it wasn't only Tom and me who had heard God's call, but our children had also. Being in the center of God's will isn't always easy, but it is guaranteed to be the most satisfying.

Back to the story. Naomi must have been one terrific mother-in-law. The affection and love shown by both daughters-in-law and also Ruth's loyalty certainly demonstrated that. Naomi, however, had hit some serious storms in the past years. The death of her husband and two sons sent her into a self-pity tailspin. Please, don't misunderstand me. I don't mean to sound insensitive or calloused, but listen to her words in Ruth 1:19-21:

> *So the two women went on until they came to Bethlehem. When they arrived in Bethlehem, the whole town was stirred because of them, and the women exclaimed, "Can this be Naomi?"*
>
> *"Don't call me Naomi," she told them. "Call me Mara, because the Almighty has made my life very bitter. I went away full, but the Lord has brought me back empty. Why call me Naomi? The Lord has afflicted me; the Almighty has brought misfortune upon me."*

Naomi had been through a tremendous loss. I can't begin to know her grief. I've never been a widow, but I did ask a few of them how they felt. Their comments were very similar. They said, "I'm so lonely," "I don't fit in with our 'couple' friends anymore," and the worst one was, "Part of me is missing." Their pain was excruciating. Their sadness was real, but sadness, when not directed to the Lord for comfort, will end in blaming and bitterness. Satan thrives on that because then we do not see the "Light" of day. Darkness sets in. Bitterness will eventually lead to hatred, and hatred destroys. Sin compounds itself.

Naomi wanted her name changed to Mara (which meant "bitter"), *"because the Almighty has made my life very bitter."* I searched and searched the book of Ruth, and no one ever did refer to her as Mara. Apparently God did not let her get away with that one.

The storms of our lives are horrible. When they hit, "self" is primed to attempt to deal with them. But God knows how to take those storms and build our faith. It's during those dark storms that He shows Himself and the way He works in such a real and personal way. If only Naomi had been as fortunate as we are to have had God's Word, she would have found comfort in these verses:

> *He who dwells in the shelter of the Most High will rest in the shadow of the Almighty. I will say of the Lord, "He is my refuge and my fortress, my God, in whom I trust" (Psalm 91:1-2).*

and

> *"The Lord himself goes before you and will be with you; he will never leave you nor*

forsake you. Do not be afraid; do not be discouraged" (Deuteronomy 31:8).

or

God is our refuge and strength, an ever-present help in trouble. Therefore we will not fear, though the earth give way and the mountains fall into the heart of the sea, though its waters roar and foam and the mountains quake with their surging (Psalm 46:1-3).

There's more:

My soul finds rest in God alone; my salvation comes from him. He alone is my rock and my salvation; he is my fortress, I will never be shaken (Psalm 62:1-2).

We are so privileged to have these powerful verses at our fingertips to give us His strength when we need it!

Believe me, there are many more verses like those that get our eyes off the storm and onto Him. Remember, storms don't last forever. Hold on, God's child. Weeping lasts for the night, but joy is promised in the morning (Psalm 30:5). We can't always change the circumstances, but we can change our attitude by looking to the source of all comfort, peace, and joy—JESUS.

Never forget, even during the storms, His plan for us is on-going. Read these assurances from God's Word:

*All the days ordained for me were written in
your book before one of them came to be
(Psalm 139:16b).*

*"For I know the plans I have for you,"
declares the Lord, "plans to prosper you
and not to harm you, plans to give you
hope and a future. Then you will call upon
me and come and pray to me, and I will
listen to you. You will seek me and find me
when you seek me with all your heart"
(Jeremiah 29:11-13).*

There is not one second that we are not in His
care. Let God be God. Trust Him. Seek Him and find
that He is all He claims to be.

God's plan for Naomi and Ruth would soon
unfold. Though the future can look so bleak and hopeless
to human eyes, God is always up to something—
something for our good. For Ruth, it was Boaz.

The two women had arrived back in Bethlehem at
barley harvest time. To support the two of them, under
God's leading Ruth offered to go to the fields of Naomi's
relative, Boaz, and glean the fields behind the harvesters
to gather any leftovers. That was a very lowly job, but
she had promised to take care of her mother-in-law, so
she submitted herself to it—not half-heartedly, either.

She first asked permission and then worked
steadily from morning until early evening.

When Boaz, who was the owner of the field and
the boss, arrived from Bethlehem, he greeted his

harvesters with, *"The Lord be with you!"* They called back, *"The Lord bless you!"* (Ruth 2:4). What a marvelous working relationship between employer and employee. To have that kind of sweet spirit atmosphere at the work place seems next to impossible, or at least like something found in a storybook. But from what we read from this story, it is possible.

I found a verse in Colossians 3:23. If that verse were followed today, there would be a different attitude in the work force all over the world.

> *Whatever you do, work at it with all your heart, as working for the Lord, not for men....*

When the Lord is the primary focus, there is no room for competition, jealousy, or a critical spirit.

Boaz noticed Ruth and inquired about her. He was moved by her willingness to serve. He immediately had compassion and a sense of responsibility for her. She honestly had no idea why he was so nice to her. Boaz knew how she had sacrificed her life for Naomi's, but she was totally oblivious to God's kindness and goodness flowing out of her. When we're filled with the Holy Spirit, we're touching lives and we might not even know it. That's when He does His best work. Ruth was gushing with the touch of God's Spirit, and she didn't even realize it. She was so genuine. What a glorious attribute. Now Ruth would begin to see the providing hand of God.

Boaz gave orders to his men:

*"Even if she gathers among the sheaves,
don't embarrass her. Rather, pull out some
stalks for her from the bundles and leave
them for her to pick up, and don't rebuke
her" (Ruth 2:15b-16).*

Oh, do you see all those intricate, well-planned details orchestrated by the Lord? There can be no one better directing the hearts involved in a romance than God. After all, He is the Author of love.

When Ruth got home and told Naomi the whole story, the reader can feel the change in Naomi take place. It was gradually dawning on her that God was providing for Ruth and her, and Boaz was to be the answer.

She worked out a plan that was culturally correct for Ruth to gain the respect, acceptance, and love of Boaz. The plan was carried out, but most importantly, the Lord was in the middle of it all.

Boaz and Ruth were married. They became the parents of Obed, who became the father of Jesse, who was the father of David. David was the man after God's own heart, whose seed led to Jesus—the Savior of the world.

What a lesson on loyalty, God's calling, following His will, and the danger of self-pity. But most of all, it shows us how our loving God will turn our sorrow into joy if we just go to Him, watch, and wait. God will never, never let us down.

6

HANNAH

After asking many people about their experiences in life, I'm confident in stating that life never goes entirely the way we planned. We all have our goals and dreams, but somewhere in the courses of our lives the Lord charts different directions for us. We have two choices when that happens. We can be bitter, or we can accept His will. Submitting to God's will is seldom easy, but when we seek the Lord for His help and guidance, we will find it is always in our best interest.

The story of Hannah shows us one of Scripture's sweetest, most sensitive, and submissive women. She was a crown jewel.

Unfortunately, we see that wrong ratio of two women to one man again and the trouble it caused. Elkanah had two wives, Peninnah and Hannah.

Year after year this man went up from his town to worship and sacrifice to the Lord Almighty at Shiloh, where Hophni and Phinehas, the two sons of Eli, were priests of the Lord. Whenever the day came for Elkanah to sacrifice, he would give portions of the meat to his wife Peninnah and to all her sons and daughters. But to Hannah he gave a double portion because he loved her, and the Lord had closed her womb. And because the Lord had closed her womb, her rival kept provoking her in order to irritate her. This went on year after year. Whenever Hannah went up to the house of the Lord, her rival provoked her till she wept and would not eat. Elkanah her husband would say to her, "Hannah, why are you weeping? Why don't you eat? Why are you downhearted? Don't I mean more to you than ten sons?" (I Samuel 1:3-8)

Neither one of the two wives had what they truly wanted. Peninnah had her sons and daughters, but not the true love she so desired from her husband. Hannah had the true love of her husband, but had no children. These two women demonstrated their real colors in the midst of disappointment.

Out of frustration and jealousy, Peninnah lashed out. Year after year, she tormented Hannah through verbal jabs and constant provoking until Hannah broke down in weeping and could not eat. The beauty of Hannah's character was evident. Even though she was very downhearted, she never sought revenge on her rival. She was miserable, and the man who knew and loved her noticed. The sad thing about this situation, however, was that he could not do a thing to make her situation better. He couldn't open her womb. He was basically helpless.

How absolutely frustrating to love someone so much, yet not be able to solve her problem for her.

The Lord allows certain struggles in our lives, the kind of struggles that no human being can solve. He does that in part to teach us and convince us that He is real and that He is definitely able to solve our problems.

I saw a billboard once that stated: "God mends broken hearts, but you have to give Him all the pieces." The key word is all. He wants our complete submissiveness and surrender. Just as a jigsaw puzzle is not complete even with only one piece missing, so also the Lord desires all the pieces to mend a broken heart.

Hannah chose to go to the Lord with all her broken pieces. Let's finish the story.

Once when they had finished eating and drinking in Shiloh, Hannah stood up. Now Eli the priest was sitting on a chair by the doorpost of the Lord's temple. In bitterness of soul Hannah wept much and prayed to the Lord. And she made a vow, saying, "O Lord Almighty, if you will only look upon your servant's misery and remember me, and not forget your servant but give her a son, then I will give him to the Lord for all the days of his life, and no razor will ever be used on his head."

As she kept on praying to the Lord, Eli observed her mouth. Hannah was praying in her heart, and her lips were moving but her voice was not heard. Eli

*thought she was drunk and said to her,
"How long will you keep on getting drunk?
Get rid of your wine."*

*"Not so, my lord," Hannah replied,
"I am a woman who is deeply troubled. I
have not been drinking wine or beer; I was
pouring out my soul to the Lord. Do not
take your servant for a wicked woman; I
have been praying here out of my great
anguish and grief."*

*Eli answered, "Go in peace, and
may the God of Israel grant you what you
have asked of him."*

*She said, "May your servant find
favor in your eyes." Then she went her way
and ate something, and her face was no
longer downcast.*

*Early the next morning they arose
and worshiped before the Lord and then
went back to their home at Ramah. Elkanah
lay with Hannah his wife, and the Lord
remembered her. So in the course of time
Hannah conceived and gave birth to a son.
She named him Samuel, saying, "Because I
asked the Lord for him" (I Samuel 1:9-20).*

I could not help but notice that all-important
phrase in the text:....*she kept on praying to the Lord....*
Hannah had a very deep personal relationship with her
God, and she wasn't about to give up. She persisted. In
fact, she prayed so intently that Eli, the priest, thought

she was drunk. Hardly! She was a hurting woman, and she was not embarrassed to admit her pain; but she certainly knew who her "Power-source" was.

As troubled as Hannah was, Eli told her to go in peace. That was very interesting. Of course, peace is from God, and He gives it even in the midst of struggle.

I remember Jesus' very own words when He spoke to His disciples. He would be leaving them. They were panicked and very troubled, but Jesus said,

> *"Peace I leave with you; my peace I give you. I do not give to you as the world gives. Do not let your hearts be troubled and do not be afraid" (John 14:27).*

We cannot produce that kind of peace ourselves, but the Holy Spirit can. Another passage of Scripture comes to mind about how to obtain this peace that Jesus said we can have. Read Philippians 4:4-7:

> *Rejoice in the Lord always. I will say it again: Rejoice! Let your gentleness be evident to all. The Lord is near. Do not be anxious about anything, but in everything, by prayer and petition, with thanksgiving, present your requests to God. And the peace of God, which transcends all understanding, will guard your hearts and your minds in Christ Jesus.*

There it is, the perfect formula for peace:

Step 1: Rejoice in the Lord always, because He is near—going through it all with us.

Step 2: Do not be anxious about anything; don't worry, because worry is not believing that God is able.

Step 3: Pray. Tell Him, but with thanksgiving. He wants us thanking Him for the answer even when we don't know what it is going to be. We just need to know it is in His hands.

On Thanksgiving Day, my pastor preached a sermon on "Giving Thanks in Everything," based on I Thessalonians 5:18, ...*give thanks in all circumstances, for this is God's will for you in Christ Jesus.*

He said that so many positive things happen when we choose to give thanks in all circumstances:

1) It keeps us aware of God's presence in our lives.

2) We are more motivated to discover God's purpose in our problems.

3) Our will bends to His will.

4) We are reminded of our complete dependence upon Jesus.

5) Our trust in God is strengthened: We don't have the answers—He does.

6) We impact our Christian witness in a positive manner because others are watching to see how we are going to deal with our circumstances.

7) Finally, we bring God glory. The Lord is lifted up rather than our problems. We

realize it is not "what" that gets us through, it's "Who."

The result: PEACE that cannot be put into words; and that peace will protect our minds from doubt and discouragement.

Hannah followed those steps and experienced real peace, and that changed her. Her circumstances had not changed, but she had. She got up and ate something. Her face was no longer downcast, and she did not even know how God was going to answer her prayer. That is what peace granted by an Almighty God will do.

Humble yourselves, therefore, under God's mighty hand, that he may lift you up in due time. Cast all your anxiety on him because he cares for you (I Peter 5:6-7).

That is so beautiful. We just have to choose to do it. Bravo, Hannah, for making that wonderful choice.

Bravo is an appropriate word—I know. A little boy from the inner-city taught me that. In a very quiet, conservative church (but he didn't know that), when I had just finished singing "Amazing Grace,"[2] that precious child shouted out "BRAVO!" Think about it. If it wasn't for all of God's love and provisions for us in our salvation and in our Christian journey, we would be a hopeless, helpless mess. The power of His grace continues on us every minute of every day. Yes, "BRAVO" is appropriate. Hannah acted on God's grace.

In I Samuel 1:19, notice that Hannah and her husband worshiped and praised the Lord before she conceived. We always have to make sure we have the order of Philippians 4 right. Our thankfulness, praise, and worship must always come first. That is our act of faith; and remember, faith pleases God.

When I pray, I always conclude my prayer in Jesus' name. That is not a simple little phrase I tag on to my prayer to let God know I'm winding it up. Hardly! When I pray in Jesus' name, I'm admitting to my heavenly Father that He's God, I'm not! It is His will I desire, not my own. I hand it over. That is a comfort to me.

Scripture is a never-ending source of comfort when we are struggling. Struggles will usually bring us to our lowest point. We are very vulnerable and weak at that point. It is sometimes very difficult to pray or to know what to pray for. No problem. Hear the words of the apostle Paul in Romans 8:26-27:

> *In the same way, the Spirit helps us in our weakness. We do not know what we ought to pray for, but the Spirit himself intercedes for us with groans that words cannot express. And he who searches our hearts knows the mind of the Spirit, because the Spirit intercedes for the saints in accordance with God's will.*

Interceding on our behalf is one of the great works of the Holy Spirit. When we submit and surrender to the

Holy Spirit, He then intercedes, knowing the Father's
will for us. That, in turn, helps us to match our desires
with the Father's. What a relief! I love that! The Father's
desires for me then turn into my desires. Perfect!

So often when our dreams and goals do not pan
out, we think our joy is gone, or at least partially gone,
because that dream would have made our joy complete.
That is not what the Bible says in John 15. Hear Jesus'
words in the first eleven verses.

> *"I am the true vine, and my Father is
> the gardener. He cuts off every branch in
> me that bears no fruit, while every branch
> that does bear fruit he prunes so that it will
> be even more fruitful. You are already clean
> because of the word I have spoken to you.
> Remain in me, and I will remain in you. No
> branch can bear fruit by itself; it must
> remain in the vine. Neither can you bear
> fruit unless you remain in me.*
>
> *"I am the vine; you are the branches.
> If a man remains in me and I in him, he
> will bear much fruit; apart from me you can
> do nothing. If anyone does not remain in
> me, he is like a branch that is thrown away
> and withers; such branches are picked up,
> thrown into the fire and burned. If you
> remain in me and my words remain in you,
> ask whatever you wish, and it will be given
> you. This is to my Father's glory, that you*

*bear much fruit, showing yourselves to be
my disciples.*
    *"As the Father has loved me, so have
I loved you. Now remain in my love. If you
obey my commands, you will remain in my
love, just as I have obeyed my Father's
commands and remain in his love. I have
told you this so that my joy may be in you
and that your joy may be complete"
(John 15:1-11).*

Our joy is complete when we remain in Jesus.
Jesus is our JOY. The final verse states the fact that
Jesus' joy may be in us, and that is what makes our joy
complete. People, circumstances, and dreams affect our
happiness, not our joy. Our joy has already been made
complete in Jesus.
    Complete means having all its parts or elements;
whole, entire, full. So, if that's the case, when Jesus
makes our joy complete, nothing or no one can add to it.
It is already full.
    The other day in a Bible study with several
women, the question came up, "What brings you joy?"
The women had no trouble giving their answers. I heard,
"my husband," "my children," "my grandchildren." As
they were voicing those reasons, I was watching the
downcast face of a young woman who wanted a child so
badly, but biologically she could not conceive. As she
listened to their answers, I could see that she had already
come to the conclusion, "If that's joy, I guess I'll never
have it completely."

I had to intervene and say to the women that as wonderful as all their reasons for joy were, believe it or not, the answers they gave only affected their happiness. Happiness depends on happenings; in belonging to Jesus our joy is complete. People and circumstances can change—that's why happiness is such a roller-coaster ride. Our Savior, Jesus, never changes. That's why our joy remains intact—always.

I went over to the young woman and put my arm around her. With the guidance provided by the Holy Spirit and with the unconditional love He produces, I shared with her that not having children would affect elements of her happiness, but as far as her joy was concerned, it was already in place and complete because of Jesus—with or without children. His love for us is so great. He's made Himself totally available to us, and apart from Him we can do nothing. Apart from Him all the happy things we experience cannot give us joy. Only with the strength of His love, joy, and peace in our heart can we rise above our difficulties.

That is why Hannah's attitude changed, even though her circumstances had not yet—she was still childless.

God's will, however, was that Hannah would be the mother of Samuel; but in the waiting process, look how much she learned. She matured through her suffering. God does have a purpose in all things.

Hannah named her son Samuel because she asked the Lord for him. (The name Samuel comes from the Hebrew expression "heard of God."[3]) She also had made a promise to the Lord that she was determined to keep:

to present her son back to the Lord and dedicate him to God's service in the temple. This, too, showed her deep devotion to the Lord. She put her "self" interest aside in order to keep that promise.

Now Eli, the priest, didn't have the greatest reputation for raising disciplined children. Putting Samuel in that kind of environment, in all probability, had to be a concern of Hannah's. Instead of using that as an excuse to go back on her promise, however, she no doubt used those first few years with her precious child to instill within him the truths of her God. That, too, is a very important lesson for us. We "rub off" on our children. What they see in us daily will have a powerful and lasting influence in their lives.

I remember growing up thinking I would NEVER be like my mom—heaven forbid! She's a terrific lady, but I certainly did not want to be like her. As years go by, my husband Tom tells me that I am turning out to be more like her by the day. In fact, after a certain reaction or comment I make, he'll call me my mom's name to make his point. Our children, more likely than not, carry our lifestyles and standards into their own homes. We have a mighty influence over our children. Can these words be said of you and me?

Hear, O Israel: The Lord our God, the Lord is one. Love the Lord your God with all your heart and with all your soul and with all your strength. These commandments that I give you today are to be upon your hearts. Impress them on your children. Talk about them when you sit at home and when you walk along the road, when you lie down and when you get up. Tie them as symbols on your hands and bind them on your foreheads. Write them on the doorframes of your houses and on your gates (Deuteronomy 6:4-9).

The big question I must ask myself is, "How can I give my sons what I don't have?" I find that the best and most important thing I can do for my boys is to personally love Jesus with all of my heart so that His character radiates out of me. Another very important tool I have is prayer. Especially now that they are grown and making their own decisions, instead of preaching, I pray. I give them to the Lord on a daily basis. What a reassurance that is—to place two of my most prized possessions into the hands of the Sovereign God and trust His perfect will for their lives.

As we move into the second chapter of I Samuel, we have the privilege of "hearing" Hannah's song of prayer and praise. It is so obvious that her eyes were off herself and on the Lord. It had to hurt her to give up her son as she did. Yet, her praise was sincere and glorifying to her God, who gave her complete satisfaction and fulfillment. She praised Him for who He was to her. She praised Him for His character, His holiness, His unchangeableness, His absolute knowledge of the motive behind every action, and His power which gives victory to the weak who look to Him.

We all long to be completely satisfied and fulfilled. Jesus knows that, and He explains how we can experience it. As our physical bodies need bread, water, and light to be satisfied, our hearts need Jesus to be completely satisfied. We need to look nowhere else. He is the Bread of Life (John 6:35); He is the Living Water (John 7:37-38); and He is the Light of the World (John 8:12).

Hannah experienced all of that. The proof is in I Samuel 2. Her heart was full, satisfied, and overflowing with praise.

She discovered that she could not outgive the Lord. Yes, she gave up her son, but the Lord allowed Samuel to be Israel's last judge, and the noblest of them all. Samuel anointed Israel's first King, Saul, and then King David. His name appears throughout the Scriptures as the Lord uses Samuel to encourage all of us.

God also blessed Hannah with five other children. Clearly, we cannot outgive God. The Lord has a way of honoring our sacrifice. You might have heard this phrase, "When the Lord closes a door, He opens a window." Not always according to our plan, but His; and His plan is always better anyway. Hannah would be one of the first to stand up and shout "Amen!" to that truth.

We can't let unfulfilled dreams and goals get us down. That's exactly where Satan wants us. The things we usually desire "here" tie us down. The Lord wants us looking up—heavenward.

I asked one of my very dear women in Bible study about her dreams and goals. She has watched her children grow up and leave the nest, watched her husband retire, and basically seen her life unfold with all of its ups and downs. Everyone in the class had admitted life does not go as we planned, but her answer was what the Lord is trying to get all of us to see. She said, "When I looked to Him and trusted Him, I found I received more than I had ever dreamed."

Isn't that just how the Lord works? We find our plans are not the best—His are. He's always up to more than we can imagine or think (Ephesians 3:20).

Our natural human desires have a non-ending drive for more and more. That will drive anyone crazy. When we surrender our goals and dreams to Him, however, we experience a contentment that only the Holy Spirit produces.

So, thank you, Hannah, for your inspiring example. You proved that giving thanks in all circumstances is possible for us, too. And we really can

Rejoice in the Lord always. I will say it again: Rejoice! (Philippians 4:4)

7

ABIGAIL

How do we handle a crisis? Does "panic," "out-of-control," or "nervous wreck" ring a bell? But under the circumstances, that is what we would expect, right? Wrong! That is another excuse Satan would like us to accept. As children of God, we do not live under our tough circumstances, but rather above them. The Lord is the One who lifts us up, because He is so much bigger, greater, and more powerful than any of our difficult circumstances. That does not mean we will never experience tough circumstances; we just have a way out. Jesus has the way of strengthening us so we do not become overwhelmed when a crisis hits.

I Samuel 25 introduces us to a wonderful woman named Abigail, and what a gal she was! She was very ordinary; however, her faith was in an extraordinary God. Abigail's circumstances did not place her in a bed of roses—quite the contrary.

I am getting more and more convinced, from experiencing life and studying God's Word, that it is during the tough circumstances that we find out about the character of God. We also find out what we really believe, and our actions are a reflection of our belief.

That is a serious thought. Abigail's life reflected the character of God, and it radiated on all who knew her.

The story begins in verses 2 and 3 by getting us acquainted with Abigail and her husband Nabal.

> *A certain man in Maon, who had property*
> *there at Carmel, was very wealthy. He had*
> *a thousand goats and three thousand sheep,*
> *which he was shearing in Carmel. His name*
> *was Nabal and his wife's name was Abigail.*
> *She was an intelligent and beautiful woman,*
> *but her husband, a Calebite, was surly and*
> *mean in his dealings (I Samuel 25:2-3).*

Obviously Abigail had numerous positive qualities. I wish we could say the same about Nabal. Surly means being rude, ill-tempered, and unfriendly. From that definition, I feel pretty safe in saying that he was probably quite loud, boisterous, and obnoxious, and he took pride in being a big shot. Abigail's life was not easy. Nabal was no prize.

Relationships are wonderful at their best, but they can be very difficult—especially when they involve the people we live with.

I am reminded of one grand lady, a true and beloved friend, whose life has been a radiant testimony for Jesus despite her very difficult living circumstances. Her husband got involved with pornography and an immoral lifestyle. She experienced grief and heartbreak day after day. Instead of turning to self-pity and bitterness, she turned to the Lord through prayer. Many others have been loved and prayed for by this precious saint, who sought her Lord for her fulfillment. Her spiritual life grew and grew in spite of adversity. My friend's life has been very productive for His kingdom.

What a difference when we choose Jesus rather than bitterness. Jesus gives life abundantly; bitterness destroys absolutely.

But how and why do these tough circumstances happen? When couples get married, sometimes they find very unpleasant "skeletons in the closet" that they had no idea were there. Or, maybe in the course of the relationship, one of them falls away from the Lord and changes—really changes. I often hear this statement: "That is not the person I married." Another reason, the most serious of them all, is that one of them never had a personal relationship with the Lord in the first place. The apostle Paul has terrific and serious advice on that very subject.

> *Do not be yoked together with unbelievers. For what do righteousness and wickedness have in common? Or what fellowship can light have with darkness? What harmony is there between Christ and Belial? What does a believer have in common with an unbeliever? What agreement is there between the temple of God and idols? For we are the temple of the living God. As God has said: "I will live with them and walk among them, and I*

*will be their God, and they will be my
people."*

*"Therefore come out from them and
be separate, says the Lord.*

*Touch no unclean thing, and I will
receive you."*

*"I will be a Father to you, and you
will be my sons and daughters, says the
Lord Almighty" (II Corinthians 6:14-18).*

When one person in a relationship wants to live his
or her life for the Lord because he or she loves Him, but
the other one does not even KNOW Him, it is guaranteed
that they will tangle.

A relationship should always be changing. But
what a difference when we change because we are
becoming more and more like Jesus rather than more and
more like our natural, sinful, human selves. The way we
change is our choice. When we choose to allow the Holy
Spirit to produce His fruit of unconditional love, joy,
peace, patience (long suffering and forgiveness),
kindness, goodness, faithfulness, gentleness and self-
control, that is when we experience a glorious, positive
change.

I saw that in my friend, and I saw it in Abigail. In
the middle of tough circumstances, they both
demonstrated a confidence in their God that only He can
produce.

We will go into Abigail's godly character more
later; but first, in the next verses, let's read a bit more
about Nabal and how he did business.

> *While David was in the desert, he heard that Nabal was shearing sheep. So he sent ten young men and said to them, "Go up to Nabal at Carmel and greet him in my name. Say to him: 'Long life to you! Good health to you and your household! And good health to all that is yours!*
>
> *"'Now I hear that it is sheep-shearing time. When your shepherds were with us, we did not mistreat them, and the whole time they were at Carmel nothing of theirs was missing. Ask your own servants and they will tell you. Therefore be favorable toward my young men, since we come at a festive time. Please give your servants and your son David whatever you can find for them.'"*
>
> *When David's men arrived, they gave Nabal this message in David's name. Then they waited.*
>
> *Nabal answered David's servants, "Who is this David? Who is this son of Jesse? Many servants are breaking away from their masters these days. Why should I take my bread and water, and the meat I have slaughtered for my shearers, and give it to men coming from who knows where?"*
> *(I Samuel 25:4-11)*

Because David had protected Nabal's men and flocks, he now expected hospitality in return. Only lamebrain Nabal would come up with a ridiculous question like, "*Who is this David?*" Where had Nabal been—somewhere with his head in the sand? Everyone else was aware of the fact that David was only the future king of Israel! Not a smart move, Nabal.

Read David's reaction in I Samuel 25:12-13:

> *David's men turned around and went back. When they arrived, they reported every word. David said to his men, "Put on your swords!" So they put on their swords, and David put on his. About four hundred men went up with David, while two hundred stayed with the supplies.*

and verses 21-22:

> *David had just said, "It's been useless—all my watching over this fellow's property in the desert so that nothing of his was missing. He has paid me back evil for good. May God deal with David, be it ever so severely, if by morning I leave alive one male of all who belong to him!"*

Saying that David was mad or angry is an understatement; he was livid and irrational. David was determined to bring down this punk and his whole household.

When one of Nabal's servants got wind of what had happened, he knew disaster was hanging over their heads. Just look to whom he goes with the information about Nabal's reaction to David's greeting.

> *One of the servants told Nabal's wife Abigail: "David sent messengers from the desert to give our master his greetings, but he hurled insults at them. Yet these men were very good to us. They did not mistreat us, and the whole time we were out in the fields near them nothing was missing. Night and day they were a wall around us all the time we were herding our sheep near them. Now think it over and see what you can do, because disaster is hanging over our master and his whole household. He is such a wicked man that no one can talk to him"* (I Samuel 25:14-17).

The true colors of a person do come out eventually—both good and bad. We might be able to mask the real us, for whatever the reason, for an hour or two a week, but it is just a matter of time before the real us bares itself through some word or deed. In these verses, we see the real colors of Nabal and what his servants thought of him. We also see what the household really thought of Abigail. It was obvious they loved, admired, respected, and trusted her. They depended on her to use her head, because they were sure Nabal wouldn't use his.

This was a crisis—a major one. Only Abigail kept a level head and did something about it.

Abigail lost no time. She took two hundred loaves of bread, two skins of wine, five dressed sheep, five seahs of roasted grain, a hundred cakes of raisins and two hundred cakes of pressed figs, and loaded them on donkeys. Then she told her servants, "Go on ahead; I'll follow you." But she did not tell her husband Nabal.

As she came riding her donkey into a mountain ravine, there were David and his men descending toward her, and she met them (I Samuel 25:18-20).

and verses 23-31:

When Abigail saw David, she quickly got off her donkey and bowed down before David with her face to the ground. She fell at his feet and said: "My lord, let the blame be on me alone. Please let your servant speak to you; hear what your servant has to say. May my lord pay no attention to that wicked man Nabal. He is just like his name—his name is Fool, and folly goes with him. But as for me, your servant, I did not see the men my master sent.

"Now since the Lord has kept you, my master, from bloodshed and from avenging yourself with your own hands, as surely as the Lord lives and as you live, may your enemies and all who intend to

harm my master be like Nabal. And let this gift, which your servant has brought to my master, be given to the men who follow you. Please forgive your servant's offense, for the Lord will certainly make a lasting dynasty for my master, because he fights the Lord's battles. Let no wrongdoing be found in you as long as you live. Even though someone is pursuing you to take your life, the life of my master will be bound securely in the bundle of the living by the Lord your God. But the lives of your enemies he will hurl away as from the pocket of a sling. When the Lord has done for my master every good thing he promised concerning him and has appointed him leader over Israel, my master will not have on his conscience the staggering burden of needless bloodshed or of having avenged himself. And when the Lord has brought my master success, remember your servant. "

How did she do that? She did not panic; she did not fall to pieces; she handled it. She lost no time getting everything organized, and she had never taken a class on time management, either. God is the master of time.

Again I remind you, Abigail was not superwoman. She was an ordinary human being, but she had God's character living through her. James 1:5-6 explicitly explains how she did it.

*If any of you lacks wisdom, he should ask
God, who gives generously to all without
finding fault, and it will be given to him.
But when he asks, he must believe and not
doubt, because he who doubts is like a
wave of the sea, blown and tossed by the
wind.*

We, on our own, never know how to handle a
particular crisis in just the right manner, but God
does—so ask Him. We have to be careful, though. James
goes on to tell us that there are two kinds of wisdom.

*Who is wise and understanding
among you? Let him show it by his good
life, by deeds done in the humility that
comes from wisdom. But if you harbor
bitter envy and selfish ambition in your
hearts, do not boast about it or deny the
truth. Such "wisdom" does not come down
from heaven but is earthly, unspiritual, of
the devil. For where you have envy and
selfish ambition, there you find disorder and
every evil practice.*

*But the wisdom that comes from
heaven is first of all pure; then peace-
loving, considerate, submissive, full of
mercy and good fruit, impartial and
sincere. Peacemakers who sow in peace
raise a harvest of righteousness
(James 3:13-18).*

There is earthly wisdom that fuels our own selfish ambition. It is the wisdom that worldly magazines and television, for example, want to feed to our minds and make us believe. The pull to that wisdom is great. It is so inviting and exciting, but the end result is evil.

Then there is godly wisdom that comes straight out of heaven itself. This is the wisdom we obtain from praying and studying Scripture—God's Word. One cannot help but see the contrasting results that James describes.

Abigail displayed godly wisdom down to the last detail, and it is a good thing, too. Lives were at stake. If God had not guided her completely, emotions would have run rampant, and who knows the damage that would have been done. The Lord helped Abigail control her God-given womanly emotions, and that produced positive results.

David, however, was another story. His emotion of anger was out of control. Yes, he had just cause to be angry. Anger in itself is not the sin, but when it overcomes us or possesses us, that is when it becomes a big problem. Hear how the Bible instructs us:

> *A fool gives full vent to his anger, but a wise man keeps himself under control (Proverbs 29:11).*

> *"In your anger do not sin": Do not let the sun go down while you are still angry, and do not give the devil a foothold (Ephesians 4:26-27).*

Emotions out of control give Satan just the ammunition he needs to shoot us down. James also provides instruction:

> *My dear brothers, take note of this: Everyone should be quick to listen, slow to speak and slow to become angry, for man's anger does not bring about the righteous life that God desires (James 1:19-20).*

Unchecked anger does not bring out the best in us—just the opposite—and, like all sin, it spirals us downward into worse action.

Not only did the Lord help Abigail to organize, but He also gave her a submissive heart and attitude, with a gentle and loving tone to match. This certainly was an asset in dealing with the out-of-control and soon-to-be-king, David. She handled this man beautifully. She used no tricks or manipulation, just the truth and a confidence in her God. The Holy Spirit not only gives us the right words to say, but He also shows us how to say them in a manner that is accepting, not condemning.

Abigail's wisdom came from God Himself through the power of His Spirit. There is no other explanation. She absolutely could not have handled this all-important crisis on her own. Remember, Abigail was just a mere mortal.

That is very encouraging to me. In a day and age when words are so potent, we can find comfort in a loving God who will help us with the words that roll off our tongues—if we let Him. Words can make or break, restore or kill a relationship. I suppose that is why James comes down on us pretty heavy in Chapter 3:3-12:

When we put bits into the mouths of horses to make them obey us, we can turn the whole animal. Or take ships as an example. Although they are so large and are driven by strong winds, they are steered by a very small rudder wherever the pilot wants to go. Likewise the tongue is a small part of the body, but it makes great boasts. Consider what a great forest is set on fire by a small spark. The tongue also is a fire, a world of evil among the parts of the body. It corrupts the whole person, sets the whole course of his life on fire, and is itself set on fire by hell.

All kinds of animals, birds, reptiles and creatures of the sea are being tamed and have been tamed by man, but no man can tame the tongue. It is a restless evil, full of deadly poison.

With the tongue we praise our Lord and Father, and with it we curse men, who have been made in God's likeness. Out of the same mouth come praise and cursing. My brothers, this should not be. Can both fresh water and salt water flow from the same spring? My brothers, can a fig tree bear olives, or a grapevine bear figs?

Neither can a salt spring produce fresh water.

Oh, the tongue—that tiny little mechanism can get us into so much trouble. Maybe it seems like an impossibility to keep that little baby on the straight and narrow. We try so hard, but it is no use. Although it is true that we will never totally tame the tongue, it is our responsibility to control it. The tongue is ruled by the heart, so we never have to be concerned about what comes out of our mouths when we know what is in our hearts. The contents of our hearts must be examined and revised continuously, that's for sure. Abigail's heart's desire was pure, so the overflow from her mouth was exactly what the Lord desired. That is why she knew what to say and how to say it.

When we are in need of confidence to determine what to say or how to say it, these Scripture verses are most reassuring:

Whether you turn to the right or to the left, your ears will hear a voice behind you, saying, "This is the way; walk in it" *(Isaiah 30:21).*

"But blessed is the man who trusts in the Lord, whose confidence is in him. He will be like a tree planted by the water that sends out its roots by the stream. It does not fear when heat comes; its leaves are always green. It has no worries in a year of

*drought and never fails to bear fruit"
(Jeremiah 17:7-8).*

*Let us then approach the throne of grace
with confidence, so that we may receive
mercy and find grace to help us in our time
of need (Hebrews 4:16).*

Aren't you relieved that those promises are in God's Word for us to claim? I know I am!

Abigail walked in confidence. She knew she could not change David, but God could. She simply got David's focus off himself (that will blur anyone's vision) and back to clearly looking on the Lord.

Praise the Lord! David listened to Abigail and saw the light. He realized how much he would have lost if Abigail had not stepped in.

*David said to Abigail, "Praise be to
the Lord, the God of Israel, who has sent
you today to meet me. May you be blessed
for your good judgment and for keeping me
from bloodshed this day and from avenging
myself with my own hands. Otherwise, as
surely as the Lord, the God of Israel, lives,
who has kept me from harming you, if you
had not come quickly to meet me, not one
male belonging to Nabal would have been
left alive by daybreak."*

*Then David accepted from her hand
what she had brought him and said, "Go*

*home in peace. I have heard your words
and granted your request "
(I Samuel 25:32-35).*

By her godly behavior, Abigail rescued everyone.
Unfortunately, Abigail had to go home and tell
Nabal all that had transpired. She made one attempt, but
Nabal was drinking himself into a drunken stupor, so she
knew it was senseless to try to communicate with him
then. In the morning, however, when he was sober, she
faced him. She was not alone. God was with her (He's
always there). That was once again the source of her
confidence. Otherwise, facing Nabal would have
unnerved her. She knew Nabal was a fool, and fools are
notorious for doing the foolish:

> *The fool says in his heart, "There is no
> God." They are corrupt, their deeds are
> vile; there is no one who does good
> (Psalm 14:1).*

But Abigail also knew she wasn't a fool. She stood
up to him with the truth—not revenge. Revenge is God's
job, and does He ever know the perfect way to deal with
the wicked!

> *When Abigail went to Nabal, he was in the
> house holding a banquet like that of a king.
> He was in high spirits and very drunk. So
> she told him nothing until daybreak. Then
> in the morning, when Nabal was sober, his*

wife told him all these things, and his heart failed him and he became like a stone. About ten days later, the Lord struck Nabal and he died (I Samuel 25:36-38).

Our problem people are not always zapped out of our lives just like that. But, those problem people and their actions are known by God. In His time He will handle them all. We must wait for Him because His ways are the best. Then there are no regrets on our part because we allowed Him to do it His way. From David's own pen, we read his words in Psalm 1:

Blessed is the man who does not walk in the counsel of the wicked or stand in the way of sinners or sit in the seat of mockers.

But his delight is in the law of the Lord, and on his law he meditates day and night.

He is like a tree planted by streams of water, which yields its fruit in season and whose leaf does not wither. Whatever he does prospers.

Not so the wicked! They are like chaff that the wind blows away.

Therefore the wicked will not stand in the judgment, nor sinners in the assembly of the righteous.

> *For the Lord watches over the way of*
> *the righteous, but the way of the wicked*
> *will perish.*

He always has the final say.

Believe it or not, God's people always win, but He demands our patience and trust in His will and plan for us.

> *When David heard that Nabal was*
> *dead, he said, "Praise be to the Lord, who*
> *has upheld my cause against Nabal for*
> *treating me with contempt. He has kept his*
> *servant from doing wrong and has brought*
> *Nabal's wrongdoing down on his own*
> *head."*
>
> *Then David sent word to Abigail,*
> *asking her to become his wife. His servants*
> *went to Carmel and said to Abigail, "David*
> *has sent us to you to take you to become his*
> *wife."*
>
> *She bowed down with her face to the*
> *ground and said, "Here is your*
> *maidservant, ready to serve you and wash*
> *the feet of my master's servants." Abigail*
> *quickly got on a donkey and, attended by*
> *her five maids, went with David's*
> *messengers and became his wife*
> *(I Samuel 25:39-42).*

God knows all, sees all, is over all, and has the final say in it all. The sooner we learn that the better. Abigail did, and what a gal she was. We are grateful to her for being such an outstanding role model. Hey, if she can avoid panic in the time of crisis, if she can seek God's way and God's wisdom, so can I and so can you. We serve the same awesome God! Praise His Name!

8

THE SHUNAMMITE WOMAN

Maybe this special woman is not quite as well known or familiar as some of the others, but I am very grateful her story is included in the infallible Word of God. She sparks off many lessons for the women of today.

We do not even know her name, but it doesn't take long to form a mental picture of her personality, her surroundings, and her situations.

> *One day Elisha went to Shunem. And a well-to-do woman was there, who urged him to stay for a meal. So whenever he came by, he stopped there to eat. She said to her husband, "I know that this man who often comes our way is a holy man of God. Let's make a small room on the roof and put in it a bed and a table, a chair and a lamp for him. Then he can stay there whenever he comes to us."*
>
> *One day when Elisha came, he went up to his room and lay down there. He said to his servant Gehazi, "Call the*

*Shunammite. " So he called her, and she
stood before him. Elisha said to him, "Tell
her, 'You have gone to all this trouble for
us. Now what can be done for you? Can we
speak on your behalf to the king or the
commander of the army?'"*

*She replied, "I have a home among
my own people. "*

*"What can be done for her?" Elisha
asked.*

*Gehazi said, "Well, she has no son
and her husband is old. "*

*Then Elisha said, "Call her. " So he
called her, and she stood in the doorway.
"About this time next year, " Elisha said,
"you will hold a son in your arms. "*

*"No, my lord, " she objected. "Don't
mislead your servant, O man of God!"*

*But the woman became pregnant,
and the next year about that same time she
gave birth to a son, just as Elisha had told
her (II Kings 4:8-17).*

Scripture is very clear that this woman was
materialistically well off and brimming over with
hospitality. She was very willing to share what she had
with Elisha. She understood that he and his servant
needed a place they could call home—a place to hang
their hats.

As I read this story, I could relate to it in a small
way. In our ministry, we have to "hit the road" many

days at a time. That is very difficult because I love to stay at home. Yet I know that for the work God has called us to do, it is not always possible.

Travel always looks so adventuresome to the one who never goes anywhere, but for the traveler, it is not always what it is cracked up to be. Traveling by air has its ups and downs (no pun intended). Yes, you do get to your destination more quickly, and usually it is wonderful. But every once in a while there is a delay, cancellation, mechanical problem, or weather conditions that throw off all your scheduling. I don't mean to sound like a bah-humbug traveler, but it does have it's drawbacks; and there is nothing the helpless traveler can do about it.

There is also the matter of losing luggage. I was on my way to begin a ten-day tour in California, and for the first time in my life I decided to pack EVERYTHING in one huge suitcase. It was stolen somewhere on the way to California never to be seen again. I guess that's all part of living on tour.

Most of our traveling, however, is done by car. I really praise the Lord for the thousands of miles we have safely put on our various vehicles. We have witnessed His protection over us. We know He has traveled with us every mile. But, like many who are on the highways and byways, we have our share of blow-outs, mechanical difficulties, white-knuckle weather conditions, and getting lost. He's been with us during those times as well, and we have watched Him work us out of trouble every time to see that we arrive safely at the next location.

When we get to our destination, we usually stay in people's homes. This is where we have experienced gracious hospitality. There are so many loving and giving people across the country who are willing to let us stay in their homes and prepare our meals for us. I shudder to think of what we would have done without them throughout the years. Many times we develop lasting friendships. I sometimes wonder if they are angels unaware.

I must say that the tours we take that demand us to be in a different city every night are the hardest. Every night we are in a different bed. Also, living out of a suitcase is very grueling. So, in a small way, I understand why it meant so much to Elisha that every time he passed through, this selfless woman opened up her home, even to the point of making a room for him. I know it was not "home home," but it was a place he could call his own—a private place to kick off his sandals and relax. It was his haven—a safe, comfortable refuge.

When dear people like the Shunammite woman give of themselves in humble hospitality, they have no idea of their powerful impact on a ministry. That is why Elisha wanted to give her something in return to express his gratitude.

When the request was made regarding what could be done for her, she could not come back with an answer. In human resources, she had everything she wanted, and she really didn't feel there was a need for special favors.

Elisha persisted, though. He was determined to reciprocate in some way. Elisha's servant found out that she did not have any children, and it did not look like that was a possibility either, because her husband was growing old.

Elisha, being the great prophet of God, knows that the word "impossible" is not in the Lord's vocabulary. So, he informed her that by this same time next year she would be holding a son in her arms.

It must have been a deep but silent desire for her because she did not even want the idea thrown around. No way did she want her hopes built up. But, it happened! She had her son.

What a beautiful story. Or it would have been if it had just ended there and they all had lived happily ever after. In reality (we're not talking fairy tales here), does that happen? Most of the time, not. The Lord often has other plans, because He has lessons to teach us. These lessons are all part of getting to know Him better and getting to know what He is capable of doing.

The child grew, and one day he went out to his father, who was with the reapers. "My head! My head!" he said to his father. His father told a servant, "Carry him to his mother." After the servant had lifted him up and carried him to his mother, the boy sat on her lap until noon, and then he died. She went up and laid him on the bed of the man of God, then shut the door and went out.

She called her husband and said, "Please send me one of the servants and a

*donkey so I can go to the man of God
quickly and return."*

*"Why go to him today?" he asked.
"It's not the New Moon or the Sabbath."*

"It's all right," she said.

*She saddled the donkey and said to
her servant, "Lead on; don't slow down for
me unless I tell you." So she set out and
came to the man of God at Mount Carmel.*

*When he saw her in the distance, the
man of God said to his servant Gehazi,
"Look! There's the Shunammite! Run to
meet her and ask her, 'Are you all right? Is
your husband all right? Is your child all
right?'"*

"Everything is all right," she said.

*When she reached the man of God at
the mountain, she took hold of his feet.
Gehazi came over to push her away, but the
man of God said, "Leave her alone! She is
in bitter distress, but the Lord has hidden it
from me and has not told me why."*

*"Did I ask you for a son, my Lord?"
she said. "Didn't I tell you, 'Don't raise my
hopes'?"* (II Kings 4:18-28)

When we first read these verses, we can't help but
respond, "Now that doesn't make any sense at all. Why
would the Lord bless her with a son to take him away?"
The Shunammite woman basically asked the same
question. In fact, she was in such bitter distress that she

started blaming and accusing Elisha for all of this. She had never asked for the child, and in so many words she said that if Elisha had listened to her she never would have had the child. Then she would have never had to go through that pain of losing him.

I know a very special couple who, unfortunately, went through that same experience. They wanted a baby so badly, and for years they prayed that the Lord would bless them with a child. Year after year went by, and then one day she discovered she was pregnant! They were elated, to say the least, and very thankful. She gave birth to a darling, healthy baby boy.

When this living doll was three months old, I came to sing in their church. Even at three months, this child got "into" music. As I sang, I could see his little legs and arms moving up and down. He was absolutely adorable. Of course, those parents were beaming with love and pride.

I was in shock the next day when I heard that precious baby had died—very suddenly, very unexpectedly. It is suspected that the cause was the mysterious crib death (SIDS—Sudden Infant Death Syndrome). This did not, I repeat NOT make any sense. Why would the Lord give them that baby after so many years only to take him away in only three short months?

That question, I'm sure, was on the mind of every person sitting at the baby's funeral. I sang at that funeral, and when I heard my voice come forth with "His Eye is on the Sparrow, and I Know He's Watching Me,"[4] I received the answer. Not the answer to why, actually, but the answer to accept His will, because God is sovereign.

The big questions when God makes a move that doesn't make sense are, "Where is our faith?" and "What do we really believe?" If we could always see the reasons why, we would not need faith. To believe and trust when we cannot see is faith.

No one wants to go through pain and suffering. It is hard to see that God can and will turn a disaster into good for those who love Him and are called according to His purpose.

Even Jesus wanted "the cup" of humiliation and death taken from Him (Matthew 26:39) though He knew the outcome. Aren't we extremely grateful the Father said "No," knowing that Jesus' death and resurrection were the only hope for our salvation?

The sovereignty of God is a big subject. The word sovereign means having supreme rank, power, and authority, and being above all others in character, importance, and excellence. That definition really says it all. That is the position of the God we serve, and because of that position we are not to (even though we want to) question His sovereignty. He can do what He wants, when He wants, and how He wants because He is the sovereign God. We either believe that fact or not.

God is not obligated to explain Himself to us. Here's proof:

> *It is the glory of God to conceal a matter;*
> *to search out a matter is the glory of kings*
> *(Proverbs 25:2).*

The secret things belong to the Lord our God, but the things revealed belong to us and to our children forever, that we may follow all the words of this law (Deuteronomy 29:29).

As you do not know the path of the wind, or how the body is formed in a mother's womb, so you cannot understand the work of God, the Maker of all things (Ecclesiastes 11:5).

"For my thoughts are not your thoughts, neither are your ways my ways," declares the Lord.
"As the heavens are higher than the earth, so are my ways higher than your ways and my thoughts than your thoughts" (Isaiah 55:8-9).

Do you know why we don't know everything? At least part of the answer is very simple. We would not be able to understand it all, even if He told us. We lack the capacity to grasp God's infinite mind. We do not know the mind of God. Our minds, as great as they are, are very limited, and when we try to comprehend God, we are actually trying to be like God. How arrogant we get!

"For who has known the mind of the Lord that he may instruct him?" (I Cor. 2:16)

His Word also gives great comfort when answers are not there or are not clear.

> *"So do not fear, for I am with you; do not be dismayed, for I am your God. I will strengthen you and help you; I will uphold you with my righteous right hand"* *(Isaiah 41:10).*

The flip side of going to His Word to find this acceptance, comfort, and security is trying to find these things for ourselves through human means. There is nothing that tears up faith more than the confusion and disillusionment brought on by our human expectations.

God is in the business of growing our faith into maturity. He knows exactly how to do that in each individual because He knows us better than we know ourselves. I was reading in Deuteronomy 8 these verses on that subject.

> *Remember how the Lord your God led you all the way in the desert these forty years, to humble you and to test you in order to know what was in your heart, whether or not you would keep his commands. He humbled you, causing you to hunger and then feeding you with manna, which neither you nor your fathers had known, to teach you that man does not live on bread alone but on every word that comes from the mouth of the Lord (Deuteronomy 8:2-3).*

and then verse 5:

> *Know then in your heart that as a man*
> *disciplines his son, so the Lord your God*
> *disciplines you.*

That word discipline is a blinger. It means to train by instruction and exercise; drill; to bring to a state of order and obedience by training and control.

Who likes discipline? Not I! But I do like the results, and so does the Lord. So I can't help but reiterate:

> *No discipline seems pleasant at the time,*
> *but painful. Later on, however, it produces*
> *a harvest of righteousness and peace for*
> *those who have been trained by it*
> *(Hebrews 12:11).*

And it is reassuring to know that

> *My son, do not despise the Lord's discipline*
> *and do not resent his rebuke, because the*
> *Lord disciplines those he loves, as a father*
> *the son he delights in (Proverbs 3:11-12).*

So, it looks as though we are in training—not in muscle building, but rather in faith building, and it is definitely for our benefit. Faith is the essential quality in the life of a Christian. Remember, faith can move mountains. Jesus said,

... "Because you have so little faith. I tell you the truth, if you have faith as small as a mustard seed, you can say to this mountain, 'Move from here to there' and it will move. Nothing will be impossible for you" (Matthew 17:20-21).

Always keep in mind that we have an enemy (Satan), who loves to undermine our faith. He does his best work when we are vulnerable, hurting, doubting, and questioning. We have to consciously and continuously choose to believe that our faith is not anchored in signs and wonders but is anchored in a sovereign God. We then surrender to His divine authority.

We have all had a crisis or two in our lives. As we have probably experienced during those times, it is hard to grasp all of this, but time is of the essence. It is very important for us to lay a foundation of faith and trust in God before another crisis hits. If that foundation is already in place, the Holy Spirit can help us recall what we know is true, and although it might rock a little, our foundation will not crumble. It is crucial to keep our Bibles open and to be studying His words daily. The results are a stronger grounding in the very person of our sovereign God.

He is present and involved in our lives, even when He seems deaf or on an extended leave of absence. God's timing is perfect, even when He appears late. For reasons that are impossible to explain, we human beings are

incredibly precious to God. I find myself resting in that.
I feel safe in the middle of the storm.

> *A righteous man may have many troubles,*
> *but the Lord delivers him from them all*
> *(Psalm 34:19).*

The Lord always promises us a rainbow even
though we may not recognize it as such at the time. We
must choose to believe it will come. The storm does not
last forever.

> *Elisha said to Gehazi, "Tuck your*
> *cloak into your belt, take my staff in your*
> *hand and run. If you meet anyone, do not*
> *greet him, and if anyone greets you, do not*
> *answer. Lay my staff on the boy's face."*
> *But the child's mother said, "As*
> *surely as the Lord lives and as you live, I*
> *will not leave you." So he got up and*
> *followed her.*
> *Gehazi went on ahead and laid the*
> *staff on the boy's face, but there was no*
> *sound or response. So Gehazi went back to*
> *meet Elisha and told him, "The boy has not*
> *awakened."*
> *When Elisha reached the house,*
> *there was the boy lying dead on his couch.*
> *He went in, shut the door on the two of*
> *them and prayed to the Lord. Then he got*
> *on the bed and lay upon the boy, mouth to*

mouth, eyes to eyes, hands to hands. As he stretched himself out upon him, the boy's body grew warm. Elisha turned away and walked back and forth in the room and then got on the bed and stretched out upon him once more. The boy sneezed seven times and opened his eyes.

Elisha summoned Gehazi and said, "Call the Shunammite." And he did. When she came, he said, "Take your son." She came in, fell at his feet and bowed to the ground. Then she took her son and went out (II Kings 4:29-37).

I am thrilled for this woman. What a perfect ending. We do not always get our perfect endings, though, do we? And when we don't, we have two choices: 1) continue to question, doubt, turn bitter, be frustrated and miserable, or 2) choose to stand firm on the foundation of faith and trust in a sovereign God who loves us and treasures us. What a way to live:

Know therefore that the Lord your God is God; he is the faithful God, keeping his covenant of love to a thousand generations of those who love him and keep his commands (Deuteronomy 7:9).

I catch myself singing Psalm 100:

Shout for joy to the Lord, all the earth. Worship the Lord with gladness; come before him with joyful songs. Know that the Lord is God. It is he who made us, and we are his; we are his people, the sheep of his pasture.

Enter his gates with thanksgiving and his courts with praise; give thanks to him and praise his name. For the Lord is good and his love endures forever; his faithfulness continues through all generations.

He always knows what He's doing, even when we don't.

P.T.L. (Praise The Lord!)

9

ESTHER

Studying the beautiful story of Esther is like picking up a book of fairy tales and reading Cinderella. It is the story of a poor orphan girl who became a great queen.

We all know and love the fairy tales, but what are the odds of that really happening? It's only possible with the Lord is all I can say.

When people have disadvantaged beginnings, that so often becomes the excuse for poor behavior. We can choose to be victims of our circumstances.

Esther is such a powerful example for us today because, although she was a disadvantaged young woman, she rose up with inner strength. Read how her story starts out.

Now there was in the citadel of Susa a Jew of the tribe of Benjamin, named Mordecai son of Jair, the son of Shimei, the son of Kish, who had been carried into exile from Jerusalem by Nebuchadnezzar king of Babylon, among those taken captive with Jehoiachin king of Judah. Mordecai

*had a cousin named Hadassah, whom he
had brought up because she had neither
father nor mother. This girl, who was also
known as Esther, was lovely in form and
features, and Mordecai had taken her as his
own daughter when her father and mother
died (Esther 2:5-7).*

Someday in heaven I would very much like to talk
to her. She must have experienced so many tears,
questions, and emotional times, yet she rose to the
challenge and made the most of the circumstances in
which she found herself.

We are all products of our environment. We have
all had circumstances in our lives over which we have
had no control. We have a choice to either let those
uncontrollable circumstances beat us down, or like
Esther, to rise above them with the Lord's help.

In thinking about those two choices, my own
mother came to my mind. She has an Esther story. She
experienced very unfortunate and uncontrollable
beginnings. When she was nine, she lost her mother. A
nine-year-old little girl's life without a mom is frightful.
I cannot even imagine being without my mom now, let
alone at nine.

She and her two brothers and two sisters went to
live with an aunt. She was a wonderful woman, but she
was also a widow with three children of her own.

My mother's father could not raise the five
children because he had a very severe drinking problem.
In fact, my mom has told me about different times when

she was a teenager that my grandpa, when he'd had too much to drink, would get quite violent. She would have to call her boyfriend (who later became her husband and my dad), and he would have to come from way across town and forcibly get him away from my mom and calm him down.

She couldn't go to the school that her girlfriends went to because her aunt and father could not afford the expensive tuition. No one even came to see her graduate from high school.

Even though it was not true, she always felt as if she were a step below everyone else—a little like second class.

She could not help it that her mother had died, that she had to live with her aunt, and that her father was an alcoholic. She was a victim of very sad circumstances. But, she would not let those uncontrollable circumstances defeat her. She chose to make her life count for something—using no excuses. The love that she longed for but had not received, she now poured into my dad, my two brothers, and myself. She gave selflessly to us for years and continues to do so today. I very seldom head out on any singing or speaking engagement that my mom doesn't call and say, "Do good." I can always count on her encouragement, support, and belief in me.

So, instead of feeling sorry for herself, she turned those unfortunate circumstances around and became one of the greatest moms in the world. She's proved to me that there will always be circumstances in life we cannot change, but whether they defeat us or not is up to us.

As we get back to Esther, we can't help thinking that the whole book is like an exciting fictional novel with twists and turns around every corner. It would be to your benefit to read all ten chapters in their entirety because you don't want to miss a detail, but I will try to highlight the story.

God has always had His people, and this story really demonstrates that. In the middle of ungodly territory were God's chosen people—the Jews. They were under the rule of King Xerxes, who ruled 127 provinces stretching from India to Cush.

The king loved showing off at parties. So, for 180 days he displayed the vast wealth of his kingdom and the splendor and glory of his majesty to all his nobles, military leaders, officials, and princes. (Isn't that nauseating?)

King Xerxes was married to Queen Vashti. After seven days of partying and a little too much to drink, the king called for his queen to come before all the men and parade her beauty.

When she received the message, she refused to go. That was forbidden for that culture. The queen was never to refuse the king anything.

Believe me, I am not a "women's libber," but I can't blame Vashti for refusing. If the king had told her he loved her, was so very proud of her, and wanted her by his side because they were a team, that would have been another story. But just to display her physical beauty in front of a bunch of egotistical, drunk, and grabbin' men—no thanks.

The king was furious and gathered his experts to decide what to do about it. They knew that the queen's conduct would become known to all the women. They feared that would result in total discord among the women and disrespect being directed at them. So, to keep the women in their proper cultural place, they ousted Queen Vashti. She would never be allowed into the king's presence again.

The search began for a new queen. What a process! Because of her great beauty, Esther went right to the top of the list of beautiful young virgins. Already we can see God's hand guiding all the details and getting them into place. God is the controller of all things!

As she was going through her year of beauty treatments, her guardian and cousin, Mordecai, *walked back and forth near the courtyard of the harem to find out how Esther was and what was happening to her* (Esther 2:11). He took his responsibility of rearing her very seriously.

Up to this point, Esther had not revealed that she was a Jew because Mordecai had forbidden her to do so—all part of God's perfect timing.

When Esther's turn came to go to the king, he was very attracted to her and she won his favor and approval more than any of the other virgins. He made her his queen.

But there was a fly in the ointment. In this case the fly's name was Haman. He was the top official in King Xerxes' regime, and he loved every minute of his power. When Mordecai would not kneel and pay honor to Haman as he went by, Haman flew into an irrational rage. He was determined to find a way to kill not only Mordecai, but all Mordecai's people—the Jews. Big problem—Queen Esther was a Jew, but none of the officials knew it.

When Mordecai learned of Haman's plan, he sought Esther out for her help. He wanted her to appear before the king, beg for mercy, and plead with him for her people. That was not a simple or easy request. For any man or woman who approached the king in the inner court without being summoned, the king had but one law: that he or she be put to death. The only exception to this was for the king to extend the gold scepter to that person and spare his or her life.

Esther made certain Mordecai knew what she was up against. Her hands were tied. That was the law. What could she do? She knew her position as queen, but she also knew the firmness of the king's law.

Mordecai was not afraid. He had his foundation strongly laid in his God. He was experienced, strong, and stable in the Lord, and he was confident that God's plan was in motion.

Read from Esther 4:12-14 his firm response to Queen Esther.

When Esther's words were reported to Mordecai, he sent back this answer: "Do not think that because you are in the king's house you alone of all the Jews will escape. For if you remain silent at this time, relief and deliverance for the Jews will arise from another place, but you and your father's family will perish. And who knows but that you have come to royal position for such a time as this?"

Esther got the message! Her reply:

> *Then Esther sent this reply to Mordecai: "Go, gather together all the Jews who are in Susa, and fast for me. Do not eat or drink for three days, night or day. I and my maids will fast as you do. When this is done, I will go to the king, even though it is against the law. And if I perish, I perish."*
> *So Mordecai went away and carried out all of Esther's instructions (Esther 4:15-17).*

Esther had many terrific qualities, and being teachable was one of her best ones. She did not let her position as queen go to her head and then ignore all she had learned and continued to learn from her cousin Mordecai. What a team they had been and continued to be.

She changed from being a scared little girl to being a strong woman of God, stepping out of her comfort zone for what she knew was right. She knew what she had to do. Her first priority was to get a prayer group started on her behalf to back her up. She knew the power behind prayer. God's power will always be victorious over any human kingly power. If the job was going to get done, the Lord was going to have to do it. This activated within her a complete belief in her cause.

Panic comes when we look at the storm. That's enemy territory. Peace comes when we look to the One bigger than the storm. Esther looked to her God, and with that confidence she moved in faith and put the plan into action. She was now in God's territory, and in God's territory fear is changed into courage and power when we walk in trust and obedience.

I'm reminded of the invalid in John 5:1-9a:

> *Some time later, Jesus went up to Jerusalem for a feast of the Jews. Now there is in Jerusalem near the Sheep Gate a pool, which in Aramaic is called Bethesda and which is surrounded by five covered colonnades. Here a great number of disabled people used to lie—the blind, the lame, the paralyzed. One who was there had been an invalid for thirty-eight years. When Jesus saw him lying there and learned that he had been in this condition for a long time, he asked him, "Do you want to get well?"*
>
> *"Sir," the invalid replied, "I have no one to help me into the pool when the water is stirred. While I am trying to get in, someone else goes down ahead of me."*
>
> *Then Jesus said to him, "Get up! Pick up your mat and walk." At once the*

*man was cured; he picked up his mat and
walked.*

Jesus' question was wise. He knew a person needs
a desire to get well and accept the changes that come
after healing takes place. No longer would the invalid be
able to use his ailment as an excuse for defeat. Jesus
commanded him to get up. That was a test of the man's
faith. Faith is only good if it is acted upon:

*In the same way, faith by itself, if it is not
accompanied by action, is dead
(James 2:17).*

Jesus then commanded him to pick up his mat and
walk. But, sometimes we just have to accept our
circumstances the way they are and move forward
anyway. That's when we move into God's territory.

Now follow the story in Esther 5:1-8:

*On the third day Esther put on her
royal robes and stood in the inner court of
the palace, in front of the king's hall. The
king was sitting on his royal throne in the
hall, facing the entrance. When he saw
Queen Esther standing in the court, he was
pleased with her and held out to her the
gold scepter that was in his hand. So Esther
approached and touched the tip of the
scepter.*

Then the king asked, "What is it, Queen Esther? What is your request? Even up to half the kingdom, it will be given you."

"If it pleases the king," replied Esther, "let the king, together with Haman, come today to a banquet I have prepared for him."

"Bring Haman at once," the king said, "so that we may do what Esther asks."

So the king and Haman went to the banquet Esther had prepared. As they were drinking wine, the king again asked Esther, "Now what is your petition? It will be given you. And what is your request? Even up to half the kingdom, it will be granted."

Esther replied, "My petition and my request is this: If the king regards me with favor and if it pleases the king to grant my petition and fulfill my request, let the king and Haman come tomorrow to the banquet I will prepare for them. Then I will answer the king's question."

So far it has all worked out perfectly! God's providence is perfect, and we must be willing to comply with it and follow it selflessly.

You must read this now about Haman. Our God is the master of details.

Haman went out that day happy and in high spirits. But when he saw Mordecai at the king's gate and observed that he neither rose nor showed fear in his presence, he was filled with rage against Mordecai. Nevertheless, Haman restrained himself and went home.

Calling together his friends and Zeresh, his wife, Haman boasted to them about his vast wealth, his many sons, and all the ways the king had honored him and how he had elevated him above the other nobles and officials. "And that's not all," Haman added. "I'm the only person Queen Esther invited to accompany the king to the banquet she gave. And she has invited me along with the king tomorrow. But all this gives me no satisfaction as long as I see that Jew Mordecai sitting at the king's gate."

His wife Zeresh and all his friends said to him, "Have a gallows built, seventy-five feet high, and ask the king in the morning to have Mordecai hanged on it. Then go with the king to the dinner and be happy." This suggestion delighted Haman, and he had the gallows built (Esther 5:9-14).

Haman became the obstacle again. Not only did he want the Jews killed, he wanted Mordecai hung from a

75-foot high gallows to be a spectacle and a demonstration to all for not kneeling to him. He figured that he could then go to the big banquet without the dark cloud of Mordecai hanging over his head. He would be rid of him once and for all.

An EGOist is always Easing God Out. That always looks good for awhile. It makes one feel so mighty and smug, but it almost always ends like an exploding bomb. It can blow up in one's face. *Pride goes before destruction, a haughty spirit before a fall* (Proverbs 16:18).

Haman had had his heyday, but the bomb was ready to explode. God still sits on the throne.

The night before Mordecai was to hang from the gallows, the king could not sleep. He called for the book of the chronicles, the record of his reign, to be read to him. In the book he discovered that Mordecai had uncovered a conspiracy to kill him, and as a result, Mordecai had saved his life. This was yet another display of the Lord's complete control over every detail in our lives. A past event in Mordecai's life would now be instrumental in fulfilling God's perfect plan to protect His people.

Keep reading the Scripture. Just watch the story unfold.

So the king and Haman went to dine with Queen Esther, and as they were drinking wine on that second day, the king again asked, "Queen Esther, what is your petition? It will be given you. What is your request? Even up to half the kingdom, it will be granted."

Then Queen Esther answered, "If I have found favor with you, O king, and if it pleases your majesty, grant me my life—this is my petition. And spare my people—this is my request. For I and my people have been sold for destruction and slaughter and annihilation. If we had merely been sold as male and female slaves, I would have kept quiet, because no such distress would justify disturbing the king."

King Xerxes asked Queen Esther, "Who is he? Where is the man who has dared to do such a thing?"

Esther said, "The adversary and enemy is this vile Haman."

Then Haman was terrified before the king and queen. The king got up in a rage, left his wine and went out into the palace garden. But Haman, realizing that the king had already decided his fate, stayed behind to beg Queen Esther for his life.

Just as the king returned from the palace garden to the banquet hall, Haman was falling on the couch where Esther was reclining.

The king exclaimed, "Will he even molest the queen while she is with me in the house?"

> *As soon as the word left the king's mouth, they covered Haman's face. Then Harbona, one of the eunuchs attending the king, said, "A gallows seventy-five feet high stands by Haman's house. He had it made for Mordecai, who spoke up to help the king."*
>
> *The king said, "Hang him on it!" So they hanged Haman on the gallows he had prepared for Mordecai. Then the king's fury subsided (Esther 7:1-10).*

All I can say is, good or bad, usually what goes around comes around. That was true for Mordecai and Haman.

King Xerxes and Queen Esther appointed Mordecai over Haman's estate. Esther pleaded with the king to end the evil plan Haman had devised against the Jews. He did. The Jews were spared. God has always had a people.

God is just, and His justice will reign. His justice stands supreme because He is the only one who can see the heart and its motive. That is why obedience is rewarded with blessings and sin is punished. Maybe we do not see that formula working right away. It is one of those guaranteed promises from the Lord that we stand on and hold on to. That is worth remembering, especially when we are tempted to compromise, when a situation looks impossible, or when it looks like standing up for the Lord might mean you are going to lose all the way around.

I will never forget how easy it is to fall into that trap. I was doing a weekly television program with a dear sister in Christ. During the year, I could gradually see that the show was moving in a direction that challenged my scriptural beliefs and made me very uncomfortable. I loved doing that program, and I knew people were spiritually growing from it. That was my justification for staying with it. I did not want to give it up, but it was causing confusion, not only in my life, but in the lives of many who were watching. Confusion is not of the Lord. I knew what I had to do. I could not change the circumstances, so that meant I had to leave. I felt I had lost a part of me. My only consolation was that I knew I had stood true to my morals, principles, and what was right. I knew what the Lord was telling me to do; I just did not want to do it. But obedience does reap blessings. I learned a great deal from that experience, and I also know now that the window opened for me to start writing. There was not time for that before. God had that all planned and timed out perfectly. He has a way of moving His children. So,

Let us not become weary in doing good, for
at the proper time we will reap a harvest if
we do not give up (Galatians 6:9).

I count on that!

Esther was raised into royalty, and look at her human, humble, uncontrolled beginnings. Now look at our human, humble, uncontrolled beginnings; and yet with Jesus as our Lord and Savior, you and I have been raised into royalty as well.

> *Now if we are children, then we are heirs—heirs of God and co-heirs with Christ, if indeed we share in his sufferings in order that we may also share in his glory (Romans 8:17).*

Our royal wealth, courage, strength, and power do not come from or depend on this world. They are not limited or temporary, but rather limitless and eternal. As heirs to Christ, we do not have to back down from anything or anyone:

> *For God did not give us a spirit of timidity, but a spirit of power, of love and of self-discipline (II Timothy 1:7).*

and

> *Therefore, my dear brothers, stand firm. Let nothing move you. Always give yourselves fully to the work of the Lord, because you know that your labor in the Lord is not in vain (I Corinthians 15:58).*

Esther did not back down, and she allowed the Lord to use her. God has always had a people, and I pray that we are willing to allow the Lord to use us for His kingdom building. We have nothing to fear because we can do all things through Christ who strengthens us (Philippians 4:13), and He supplies us with everything we need (Philippians 4:19). Like Esther, let's be heroes for Jesus' sake.

10

MARY AND ...

I found it hard to know exactly when to stop, because there are so many women in Scripture whose stories demonstrate exactly what we need to inspire and encourage us today. My intention was to write about the examples of women from the Old Testament only; but when I started into the New Testament, the experiences of one woman after another came forth with tremendous lessons for us. Let's begin with Mary, the mother of Jesus. How could we not include her? She is one of the most monumental women in all of Scripture. Actually, she blended the women of the Old Testament into the women of the New Testament because she gave birth to the One who fulfilled the old and began the new.

It is easy to place Mary on a pedestal, but in all reality, she was just a simple, young, human woman. She possessed, however, the faithful heart that God was looking for in the mother of His Son.

An angel appeared to Mary. He told her she was highly favored and would give birth to the Son of the Most High. Naturally, she had questions. Who wouldn't?

In the sixth month, God sent the angel Gabriel to Nazareth, a town in Galilee, to a virgin pledged to be married to a man named Joseph, a descendant of David. The virgin's name was Mary. The angel went to her and said, "Greetings, you who are highly favored! The Lord is with you."

Mary was greatly troubled at his words and wondered what kind of greeting this might be. But the angel said to her, "Do not be afraid, Mary, you have found favor with God. You will be with child and give birth to a son, and you are to give him the name Jesus. He will be great and will be called the Son of the Most High. The Lord God will give him the throne of his father David, and he will reign over the house of Jacob forever; his kingdom will never end."

"How will this be," Mary asked the angel, "since I am a virgin?"

The angel answered, "The Holy Spirit will come upon you, and the power of the Most High will overshadow you. So the holy one to be born will be called the Son of God. Even Elizabeth your relative is going to have a child in her old age, and she who was said to be barren is in her sixth month. For nothing is impossible with God."

> *"I am the Lord's servant,"* Mary
> answered. *"May it be to me as you have
> said."* Then the angel left her
> *(Luke 1:26-38).*

The virgin birth: Jesus, our Savior, left the glory
of heaven to come in the form of a human baby. He
would become the only possible sacrifice of atonement
and would die for you and me.

At first, all of that looked like an impossibility to
Mary. But as the Lord had previously told Sarah in the
Old Testament, He now told Mary in the New
Testament, *"...nothing is impossible with God"* (v.37).
That is a reminder to us today and everyday.

Mary's example is impeccable. As the Lord's
servant, she totally submitted and asked no more
questions. Did she understand it all? I doubt it very
much. But, she did know her God. She clearly
demonstrated solid trust and sincere faith.

When we continue to read on in Luke 1, we see
God's sweet, understanding love for His children. When
He calls us to do anything for Him, He equips us either
with the right people or the right tools. He sent Mary to
her relative, Elizabeth. Elizabeth was also pregnant. She
was to be the mother of John the Baptist, the prophesied
forerunner of Jesus, the Savior. The Lord brought them
together so they could be a source of encouragement and
support to each other before they had to face the reality
of this harsh world's response. What an uplifting visit
they had!

As I continued to study Mary's life, I found these two verses that made me stop and think:

But Mary treasured up all these things and pondered them in her heart (Luke 2:19).

Then he went down to Nazareth with them and was obedient to them. But his mother treasured all these things in her heart (Luke 2:51).

Mary treasured and pondered her child's experiences in her heart. Memories are from God. Every moment we spend today makes a memory for tomorrow. How precious those cherished memories are, especially during hard times and after a loved one is gone.

My grandpa gave me a ring for Christmas many, many years ago. I'll never forget how I felt as he was handing out his usual dollar bills to his grandchildren. I was anxiously waiting for my $2, and he purposely ran out of money when he got to me. I was crushed. I had big plans for my money that Christmas. Then his hand went into his pocket and came out with a tiny box. I was still stewing, however, because there was no way he could have folded two dollar bills and put them into that box. "Accept it, Lynnelle, you're out the money this year," I thought.

I half-heartedly opened the box, and there lay a gorgeous little ring with two sapphire chips and a diamond chip. That setting had been awarded to him for a job well done at his work place. Instead of making it into something for himself, he had it put into a ring for me—his oldest grandchild. What a moment! What a memory! My grandpa passed away years ago, but no one can take that memory away from me.

My mom is the source of another Christmastime memory dear to my heart. Every Christmas Eve I receive a Christmas ornament from her. It is an ornament that has the date on it, but the year is always one year behind. She figures that a year or two down the road I won't remember what year I got it in anyway, so why should she pay full price for that thing. She had gotten it the day after Christmas the year before on the clearance table and saved it the whole year. My Christmas tree is full of those "corn ball" ornaments. For instance, my "Baby's First Christmas" ornament was given to me when I was 35 years old, and my "Fifty Years Together" ornament was given to me when I was 37.

Every Christmas when our tree goes up, I laugh and hug those ornaments. They will always be cherished memories that I treasure in my heart.

Mary needed those treasured moments because of what she was to face in the future. Her son's life was about to change the whole course of history:

> *On the third day a wedding took place at Cana in Galilee. Jesus' mother was there, and Jesus and his disciples had also been invited to the wedding. When the wine was gone, Jesus' mother said to him, "They have no more wine."*

"Dear woman, why do you involve me?" Jesus replied. "My time has not yet come."
His mother said to the servants, "Do whatever he tells you" (John 2:1-5).

Jesus had now begun His earthly ministry. When His mother told Him of the wine problem, He called her "dear woman." He was now Jesus the Son of God rather than Jesus the son of Mary and Joseph. Letting go of our children is never easy. Mary had to deal with more than the "empty nest." She knew her son was the Messiah. That is why she said to the servant, *"Do whatever he tells you."* How different our lives would be if we just followed her advice. We can only imagine the emotional ups and downs in Mary's life during Jesus' earthly ministry.

The hardest day of Mary's life came on the day we call Good Friday.

Near the cross of Jesus stood his mother, his mother's sister, Mary the wife of Clopas, and Mary Magdalene. When Jesus saw his mother there, and the disciple whom he loved standing nearby, he said to his mother, "Dear woman, here is your son," and to the disciple, "Here is your mother." From that time on, this disciple took her into his home (John 19:25-27).

The pain of watching Him suffer had to be more than she could bear. A mother's natural instinct is to try to fix it, but this was one time that was impossible. Jesus was now her Savior as well. What an incredibly awesome thought for that special, chosen woman of God!

Whenever one starts to read one of the gospels of Jesus, it's hard to put it down. After studying about Mary the mother of Jesus, I found the story of Jesus' friends, Mary and Martha. They were sisters with very different personalities. Mary was a quiet listener, while Martha was a vivacious doer.

Not only were their personalities different, but they had different spiritual gifts as well. God distributes these gifts perfectly. He knows the exact gift that will fit with our personality and our placement in this world.

There are different kinds of gifts, but the same Spirit. There are different kinds of service, but the same Lord. There are different kinds of working, but the same God works all of them in all men.

Now to each one the manifestation of the Spirit is given for the common good (I Corinthians 12:4-7).

All these are the work of one and the same Spirit, and he gives them to each one, just as he determines (I Corinthians 12:11).

To Him every gift is essential and equally important. Let's visit the household of Mary and Martha:

As Jesus and his disciples were on their way, he came to a village where a woman named Martha opened her home to him. She had a sister called Mary, who sat at the Lord's feet listening to what he said. But Martha was distracted by all the preparations that had to be made. She came to him and asked, "Lord, don't you care that my sister has left me to do the work by myself? Tell her to help me!"

"Martha, Martha," the Lord answered, "you are worried and upset about many things, but only one thing is needed. Mary has chosen what is better, and it will not be taken away from her" (Luke 10:38-42).

Martha's great attributes of hospitality and food preparation were God-given gifts. However, the Lord had to teach her not to let those gifts get in the way of becoming closer to Him. It is very easy to get ourselves so busy doing marvelous things for the Lord that we totally miss the personal one-on-one time vitally necessary to deepen our relationship with Him.

So, calling her by name, Jesus lovingly rebukes her. He teaches her the importance of putting Him first in her life. Is He trying to change her personality or take away her gifts? Absolutely not! He just demands top priority—first place. We all need to be taught that lesson, and it does not come easily, either. Martha learned well, and so often what we have learned will be put to the test during a crisis.

Mary and Martha's brother Lazarus fell sick. The sisters got word to Jesus, knowing He could heal him. Jesus purposely waited until after Lazarus had died before He went to them. Healing the sick was nothing new for Jesus, and all the people who followed Him were fascinated by Him. But, Jesus' time on this earth was running out. He was going to show God's glory, so the Father would be glorified through this ultimate sacrifice once and for all. He was going to do what no one else could do—raise Lazarus from the dead.

On his arrival, Jesus found that Lazarus had already been in the tomb for four days. Bethany was less than two miles from Jerusalem, and many Jews had come to Martha and Mary to comfort them in the loss of their brother. When Martha heard that Jesus was coming, she went out to meet him, but Mary stayed at home.

"Lord," Martha said to Jesus, "if you had been here, my brother would not have died. But I know that even now God will give you whatever you ask."

Jesus said to her, "Your brother will rise again."

Martha answered, "I know he will rise again in the resurrection at the last day."

Jesus said to her, "I am the resurrection and the life. He who believes in me will live, even though he dies; and whoever lives and believes in me will never die. Do you believe this?"

"Yes, Lord," she told him, "I believe that you are the Christ, the Son of God, who was to come into the world."

And after she had said this, she went back and called her sister Mary aside. "The Teacher is here," she said, "and is asking for you." When Mary heard this, she got up quickly and went to him. Now Jesus had not yet entered the village, but was still at the place where Martha had met him. When the Jews who had been with Mary in the house, comforting her, noticed how quickly she got up and went out, they followed her, supposing she was going to the tomb to mourn there.

When Mary reached the place where Jesus was and saw him, she fell at his feet and said, "Lord, if you had been here, my brother would not have died."

When Jesus saw her weeping, and the Jews who had come along with her also weeping, he was deeply moved in spirit and troubled. "Where have you laid him?" he asked.

"Come and see, Lord," they replied. Jesus wept.

Then the Jews said, "See how he loved him!"

But some of them said, "Could not he who opened the eyes of the blind man have kept this man from dying?"

Jesus, once more deeply moved, came to the tomb. It was a cave with a stone laid across the entrance. "Take away the stone," he said.

"But, Lord," said Martha, the sister of the dead man, "by this time there is a bad odor, for he has been there four days."

Then Jesus said, "Did I not tell you that if you believed, you would see the glory of God?"

So they took away the stone. Then Jesus looked up and said, "Father, I thank you that you have heard me. I knew that you always hear me, but I said this for the benefit of the people standing here, that they may believe that you sent me."

When he had said this, Jesus called in a loud voice, "Lazarus, come out!" The dead man came out, his hands and feet wrapped with strips of linen, and a cloth around his face.

Jesus said to them, "Take off the grave clothes and let him go" *(John 11:17-44).*

Can you imagine being there and watching all of that happen right before your very eyes? Our God is an awesome God! But, I'm getting ahead of myself. Let's go back to when Jesus arrived in Bethany. Did you notice who ran out to meet Him? Martha! Martha was still Martha, but Jesus was now first in her life. She was a changed woman. Jesus has a way of doing that through His teachings. Mary, however, stayed back. Sometimes our emotions can get ahead of what we believe. Whenever feelings get ahead of faith, whenever self gets into God's place (which should be first in our lives), the devil has a way of sneaking in. When we start thinking we "deserve" to feel like that, the devil puts his "d" words of discouragement, disillusionment, doubt, and depression into action. When that happens, watch God's Spirit start to wave His red warning flag.

Grief had overpowered Mary. She had a right to grieve, but not to let it overcome her. Jesus expected to see her, too, when He arrived. When she was not there with Martha, He asked about her. Martha went back and told Mary what Jesus had said. The Bible says she then got up quickly and went to Him. What caused her to move back to Jesus? Jesus' words. His Word will always move us back to Him when we have strayed away for whatever reason.

Jesus was touched by their grief. He wept. He was not grieving because of Lazarus; He knew it would be just a matter of minutes before Lazarus walked out of the tomb. He had felt their pain. His compassion reached out to all who were in mourning. What a comforting thought—to think that the Lord feels with us, hurts with us, cares tremendously about us, and yet He's the One who knows the victorious end to His children's life stories. He knows how they are all going to turn out. There isn't one little second of our lives that slips by Him. Does Jesus care? Oh yes, He most certainly does!

That is evident when Jesus met the Samaritan woman in John 4 and the woman with the sinful past in Luke 7. He moves right past what is or is not politically correct, what someone has been or is at the moment, and seeks his or her soul. Neither one of these women thought too highly of themselves. They were prime candidates for a "self-esteem build-up" seminar. There are not too many women who do not need a shot of healthy self-esteem now and then. These women, like all of us, needed to see themselves as:

1.   Fearfully and wonderfully made (Psalm 139:14):

     I praise you because I am fearfully and wonderfully made; your works are wonderful, I know that full well.

2.   Deeply fallen (Romans 3:10-12):

     As it is written: "There is no one righteous, not even one; there is no one who understands, no one who seeks God. All have turned away, they have together become worthless;

there is no one who does good, not even one."

3.   Fully forgiven (Romans 3:21-24):

But now a righteousness from God, apart from law, has been made known, to which the Law and the Prophets testify. This righteousness from God comes through faith in Jesus Christ to all who believe. There is no difference, for all have sinned and fall short of the glory of God, and are justified freely by his grace through the redemption that came by Christ Jesus.

4.   Eternally loved (Romans 8:35-39):

Who shall separate us from the love of Christ? Shall trouble or hardship or persecution or famine or nakedness or danger or sword? As it is written:

> *"For your sake we face death all day long; we are considered as sheep to be slaughtered."*

No, in all these things we are more than conquerors through him who loved us. For I am convinced that neither death nor life, neither angels nor demons, neither the present nor the future, nor any powers, neither height nor depth, nor anything else in all creation, will be able to separate us from the love of God that is in Christ Jesus our Lord.

5. Greatly blessed (Romans 10:12):

For there is no difference between Jew and Gentile—the same Lord is Lord of all and richly blesses all who call on him,...

A sincere belief in those five statements will guarantee in us a healthy self-esteem.

Notice something in those five statements. To have a great self-esteem does not require classic outward characteristics, but rather the inner working of a Spirit-filled heart. Then what radiates from our hearts reveals true beauty.

In today's world, with so much emphasis put on our outward appearance, it is a relief to know how the Lord really sees us. He is interested in the inner-self—the part of us that time cannot diminish and that will live on forever and ever.

Now don't think for a second that I am giving the green light to "let yourself go." Absolutely not! Our bodies are the temples where the Holy Spirit dwells:

> *Do you not know that your body is a temple of the Holy Spirit, who is in you, whom you have received from God? You are not your own; you were bought at a price. Therefore honor God with your body (I Cor. 6:19-20).*

I'm convinced, however, that if we take extra good care of what goes into our hearts, our bodies will automatically benefit.

It appears that the Samaritan woman and the woman with the sinful past openly responded to Jesus' offer of love. They repented of their sins, confessed Him as their Savior and Lord, and believed with their hearts. Jesus couldn't wait to forgive and save them! Their testimony radiated with the love of Jesus, and their lives affected many others. Jesus' formula for life really works.

Jesus also demonstrated His caring in the life of the sick woman in Mark 5. She had been to every kind of doctor and had spent all her money, but her sickness persisted. This dear woman was at the end of her rope. (Being at the end of our rope is not a bad place to be. Then we have nowhere else to turn but to Jesus.) It's unfortunate we wait so long to go to the Source of all sources. But we keep trying to do it on our own until the Lord does what He has to do to get our attention. She knew that if she just touched Jesus' clothes, she would be healed. She somehow worked her way through the crowd to Jesus and found out she was right. She was healed! Jesus turned to her, made her admit what she had done, and then said so beautifully to her, *"Daughter, your faith has healed you. Go in peace and be freed from your suffering"* (Mark 5:34).

Jesus cares for every one of us. Yes, He cares for the masses, but that same care is focused on us as individuals—you and me. He uses experiences from our everyday lives to demonstrate that, too.

He then expects us to demonstrate His love and care to others. We cannot forget that others are watching us. In everything we do and everywhere we go, we leave impressions on or we influence the people with whom we come in contact.

I couldn't help but see the contrast between the influence Herodias had on her daughter and the influence Eunice and Lois had on Timothy. Matthew writes an account of Herodias in chapter 14:1-12.

> *At that time Herod the tetrarch heard the reports about Jesus, and he said to his attendants, "This is John the Baptist; he has risen from the dead! That is why miraculous powers are at work in him."*
>
> *Now Herod had arrested John and bound him and put him in prison because of Herodias, his brother Philip's wife, for John had been saying to him: "It is not lawful for you to have her." Herod wanted to kill John, but he was afraid of the*

*people, because they considered him a
prophet.*

*On Herod's birthday the daughter of
Herodias danced for them and pleased
Herod so much that he promised with an
oath to give her whatever she asked.
Prompted by her mother, she said, "Give
me here on a platter the head of John the
Baptist." The king was distressed, but
because of his oaths and his dinner guests,
he ordered that her request be granted and
had John beheaded in the prison. His head
was brought in on a platter and given to the
girl, who carried it to her mother. John's
disciples came and took his body and buried
it. Then they went and told Jesus.*

That story sickens me. What a terrible example
she was to her daughter. Not only was Herodias living in
sin, but she allowed her daughter to seductively dance for
the king on his birthday. That pleased the king so much
that he promised to give the daughter whatever she
requested. Prompted by Herodias, she asked for the head
of John the Baptist on a platter. Herodias actually used
her own daughter to get rid of the man that exposed her
sinful lifestyle. I can only imagine what that influence did
to that young girl and how it affected her personally.

Now let's look at the influence and impact Eunice
and Lois had on Timothy. Paul writes these words to
Timothy:

I thank God, whom I serve, as my forefathers did, with a clear conscience, as night and day I constantly remember you in my prayers. Recalling your tears, I long to see you, so that I may be filled with joy. I have been reminded of your sincere faith, which first lived in your grandmother Lois and in your mother Eunice and, I am persuaded, now lives in you also (II Timothy 1:3-5).

Timothy must have been a wonderful young man. He had a genuine faith and a sincere heart, and Paul attributed it to his godly upbringing—the positive example and influence provided by his mother and grandmother.

What a lesson that teaches us. No, we can't pass down our faith or salvation to others, but just like Eunice and Lois, we can influence others by communicating our faith in our Lord and Savior. We should never underestimate the fact that people are watching. Do they see that our walk and talk match?

Through these women's experiences, they have shown us the character of God; and it is that same God, with that same character, who is showing Himself to us today. These women also remind us of the significance of our reactions to God's character because, sooner or later, our actions will reflect what we really believe.

Mark my words, no one loves us as much as He does. Remember, He's at work in our lives. He has plans, and He has our best interest in mind.

Many are the plans in a man's heart, but it is the Lord's purpose that prevails (Proverbs 19:21).

No one will be able to stand up against you all the days of your life. As I was with Moses, so I will be with you; I will never leave you nor forsake you (Joshua 1:5).

God and all of His sovereign authority never changes. He is the same—always has been and always will be:

Jesus Christ is the same yesterday and today and forever (Hebrews 13:8).

Point made!

CONCLUSION

Every one of these precious women of God has taught us something. They were all ordinary women, but by nature, certainly all different and unique human beings. Their successes came when they chose to plug into their Lord's power, and their failures came when they chose to plug into their own power.

In Proverbs 31, the mother of King Lemuel had some wise, sound advice for her son about what to look for in a woman. Read her advice in verses 10-31:

> *A wife of noble character who can find?*
>
> *She is worth far more than rubies.*
>
> *Her husband has full confidence in her and lacks nothing of value.*
>
> *She brings him good, not harm, all the days of her life.*
>
> *She selects wool and flax and works with eager hands.*
>
> *She is like the merchant ships, bringing her food from afar.*

She gets up while it is still dark; she provides food for her family and portions for her servant girls.

She considers a field and buys it; out of her earnings she plants a vineyard.

She sets about her work vigorously; her arms are strong for her tasks.

She sees that her trading is profitable, and her lamp does not go out at night.

In her hand she holds the distaff and grasps the spindle with her fingers.

She opens her arms to the poor and extends her hands to the needy.

When it snows, she has no fear for her household; for all of them are clothed in scarlet.

She makes coverings for her bed; she is clothed in fine linen and purple.

Her husband is respected at the city gate, where he takes his seat among the elders of the land.

She makes linen garments and sells them, and supplies the merchants with sashes.

She is clothed with strength and dignity; she can laugh at the days to come.

She speaks with wisdom, and faithful instruction is on her tongue.

She watches over the affairs of her household and does not eat the bread of idleness.

Her children arise and call her blessed; her husband also, and he praises her:

"Many women do noble things, but you surpass them all."

Charm is deceptive, and beauty is fleeting; but a woman who fears the Lord is to be praised.

Give her the reward she has earned, and let her works bring her praise at the city gate.

At first glance, you may think achieving this standard is utterly impossible. There could never be a woman that perfect. That would be wishful thinking—too good to be true. That, my friend, is where you would be wrong. You could be looking at that very woman in your mirror. How? By taking what you have learned from these biblical women and putting it into practice. Can it happen in 20 minutes? No. Probably not even in 20 years. A Proverbs 31 woman takes time. I have made it a practice, however, to reread that proverb after a period of time to see what progress I have made. The more we apply the character of God and the love of Jesus in our lives, the more we will see that portrait of excellence coming out. How and why does that happen?

*"I have been crucified with Christ and I no
longer live, but Christ lives in me"
(Galatians 2:20a).*

I am a new person and continue to be renewed day
by day as I let myself surrender to His Spirit. As God's
children, we will see a fresh newness in everything we
do, and rightly so if we are really in love with Jesus and
follow Paul's words in Romans 12:1:

*Therefore, I urge you, brothers, in view of
God's mercy, to offer your bodies as living
sacrifices, holy and pleasing to God—this is
your spiritual act of worship.*

Going back to the woman of noble godly character
in Proverbs 31, who wouldn't want to be like that? Just
look at her life; it's overflowing with stunning qualities.
She knew her place in the family system. In a godly
home, there is no power struggle because all of the
members understand their proper place in the order that
the Lord has set up for a family. Her husband faithfully
did his job and knew she was doing hers. They were
distinct individuals with distinctly different jobs, yet they
worked as a team. He had full confidence in her. They
had earned each other's mutual respect and confidence,
and those are two gorgeous qualities.

She certainly was not afraid of work. She knew
work was good for her. Too much free time is
dangerous. She was not lazy; instead she used the
resources God had given her. Everyone has to learn to

live within his or her means and use his or her resources, whether limited or not, the best way one can. My dear, wonderful, godly, perfect example of a mother-in-law has a way of taking every little amount of food she has and using it to create a feast. I marvel at her resourcefulness. We tease her that she must know Jesus' secret on how to feed the 5,000 (Mark 6:30-44).

The woman of Proverbs 31 had good judgment and was very caring and compassionate. She watched what she said and spoke with wisdom when she did speak. Her beautiful, selfless attitude and character spilled over onto her family. They were not subjected to a bickering, nagging woman who demanded her rights, space, time, and attention. Instead, they felt and experienced her endearing love for them. That was the kind of character model she was passing down to her children—her loving, lasting investment.

The secret of her praiseworthy life was the sincere and genuine relationship she had with her Lord. Her eyes were on Him for strength and endurance instead of on herself. She looked at being a wife and mother as an all-important calling from God.

Sometimes when I am doing dishes or laundry, mopping or vacuuming floors, straightening up, and so on, the old "sorry for myself" syndrome kicks in because I feel my husband and sons should be helping me. The Lord gently reminds me (again) that before time began, He knew Tom, Chad, and Jason. He knew they needed ME; I was hand picked for them. The Lord wanted no one else to be Tom's wife and Chad and Jason's mother. What a wake-up call! Now that doesn't mean that they are excused from their chores and duties, but when they slip up, I need to forgive them. (And, hey, I slip up, too, and Jesus keeps forgiving me!) Jesus is constantly whispering in my ear to focus on what is really important—the very life of my husband and boys. It's an all-important calling by God to be wife and mother to these three men, and Jesus expects me to follow it through. He'll walk right by my side all the way.

You and I know that our attitude can make or break us. An older woman approached me after a concert and honestly admitted to me that she walked into the service that morning full of self-pity. She had complained all the way to church and felt totally justified in feeling sorry for herself. She admitted she was miserable (self-contained people are). Unfortunately, everyone in the car was affected by her self-centered mood, too. One verse of "Amazing Grace"[2] convicted her. She was reminded of what Jesus had done for her. That admission and submission allowed her to activate the Holy Spirit within her, and He turned her attitude completely around. The nurturing of our attitude lies in our own hands. Our attitude can change our day and can also change a relationship.

How do we keep our eyes on the Lord's purpose for us and find complete satisfaction in that? We take time to be holy. If we do not take time, it's like saying to the Lord that we can live life without Him. We certainly know that isn't true, don't we? I'm finding myself singing the old hymn, "I Need Thee Every Hour"[5] more and more. What a comfort and relief to know that my

God is in control of every detail of my life. In fact, He is the blessed controller of all things.

Through the power of the Holy Spirit, I pray that you have been convinced that the Bible is still relevant for this very day. If it were not, what would be our reasoning for going to Scripture for teaching, correcting, training, and equipping us for every good work?

Even though this powerful, holy Book was written thousands of years ago, God knew His people—yes, even you and me. He knew exactly what guideline He wanted us to walk by and the guideline He knew we needed to walk by.

We need God's Word!

So I repeat these verses from Psalm 119:

How can a young man keep his way pure?
By living according to your word (v.9).

I have hidden your word in my heart that I might not sin against you (v.11).

Your word, O Lord, is eternal; it stands firm in the heavens. Your faithfulness continues through all generations; you established the earth, and it endures (v.89-90).

Your word is a lamp to my feet and a light for my path (v.105).

*You are my refuge and my shield; I have
put my hope in your word (v.114).*

I also offer additional support for Scripture's relevance
with this verse:

*"The grass withers and the flowers fall, but
the word of our God stands forever"
(Isaiah 40:8).*

We cannot expect to have a victorious, personal,
spiritual walk with the Lord without studying and
following His Word. When we do that, we are taking
time to be holy, and the results are phenomenal.

Well, that about wraps it up. These women have
proved that basically God's Gals Haven't Changed a Bit!
They have also proved that the Solution hasn't changed
a bit, either.

From Scripture, it has been very evident that God
has loved and has put great worth on women throughout
all of time. They have been used by God to teach others
and ultimately fulfill His purpose of bringing Jesus into
this world. Now God's purpose continues as His Word is
spread that salvation is in Jesus and Jesus alone, and the
Lord is still using His gals to do that! What a humbling,
but thrilling reality that is. My prayer is that you KNOW
that you are one of HIS gals. And as God's gals, we
know that although our bodies may be simply jars of
clay, a treasure lies within (II Corinthians 4:7)—a
treasure filled with the Spirit of God, God's words, and
confidence in our future.

> *Therefore we do not lose heart. Though outwardly we are wasting away, yet inwardly we are being renewed day by day. For our light and momentary troubles are achieving for us an eternal glory that far outweighs them all. So we fix our eyes not on what is seen, but on what is unseen. For what is seen is temporary, but what is unseen is eternal (II Corinthians 4:16-18).*

So with that instruction and promise, being one of God's gals is certainly a great way to live, and we live in the assurance and the security of knowing that God's Gals Haven't Changed a Bit!

ACKNOWLEDGMENTS

For permission to reprint copyrighted material, grateful acknowledgment is made to the following publishers:

HOLY BIBLE: NEW INTERNATIONAL VERSION®. NIV®. Copyright© 1973, 1978, 1984 by International Bible Society. Used by permission of Zondervan Publishing House. The "NIV" and "New International Version" trademarks are registered in the United States Patent and Trademark Office by International Bible Society.

Notes and Bible helps copyright© 1988, 1989, 1990, 1991 by Tyndale House Publishers, Inc., used by permission.

Barna Research. Commissioned by Tyndale House Publishers, Inc. Used by permission. All rights reserved.

REFERENCES

1. Barna Research. Commissioned by Tyndale House Publishers, Inc. Used by permission. All rights reserved.

2. Newton, John and Edwin O. Excell, "Amazing Grace!"

3. Notes and Bible helps copyright© 1988, 1989, 1990, 1991 by Tyndale House Publishers, Inc., used by permission.

4. Martin, Civilla D. and Charles H. Gabriel, "His Eye Is On The Sparrow."

5. Hawks, Annie S. and Robert Lowry, "I Need Thee Every Hour."

SCRIPTURE INDEX

STUDY GUIDE

GOD'S GALS HAVEN'T

CHANGED A BIT!

LESSON ONE: EVE
Genesis 3

1. Why is this chapter in Scripture so disastrous?

2. Who is Satan?

   What is his problem, and how does he go about solving it?

3. Why do you think doubt and discontent are still his "trump cards" today?

4. Compare the woman's answer to the serpent's question (v.1-3) with God's original instruction in Genesis 2:17.

   Explain why this is dangerous.

5. Temptation does not just happen. There is always a series of events leading to it. From this passage, list the series of events Eve experienced.

6. Eve succumbed to the temptation. The "self" attitude was born. How does this happen and what should Eve have done?

7. Do you really believe that God takes sin seriously? Explain.

8. What were the immediate consequences of sin?

9. What were the long-range consequences of sin?

10. Where do you see the promise of Jesus? (Now that's real love!)

11. From I Corinthians 10:13 and Ephesians 6:10-18, how can we beat temptation?

12. The ultimate consequence of sin is death. To save you from spiritual death, God says, "*Where are you?*" What must you do to be saved from spiritual death?

LESSON TWO: SARAH AND HAGAR
Genesis 16, 18:1-15

1. When all things look hopeless, is it easy to hang on and believe? What is faith?

2. If true faith waits for <u>God's</u> timing, why is waiting still so difficult?

3. Why does Sarah take matters into her own hands?

   At what point do you think she regrets her decision?

4. Why do you think the ratio of two women to one man will never work, culturally correct or not? (Genesis 2:24).

5. They are all in a mess. Describe the state of Sarah, Hagar, and Abraham.

6. What was Hagar's background?

   How does Hagar learn about God in her personal struggles?

   Do you think He does His best teaching during your personal struggles?

7.   What did the angel tell her to do, and why was this such a serious instruction for Hagar?

8.   Thirteen long years later, what happened?

9.   What was Sarah's reaction?

     What was the Lord's response?

10. From Genesis 18:14, what is the crucial phrase you must constantly repeat in hopeless times?

11. Reading Romans 4:18-21, why is Abraham such a great example of faith while waiting for God's promise?

12. If you believe God and His promises are real, does your lifestyle prove it?

LESSON THREE: MIRIAM
Numbers 12

1. What were Miriam and Aaron guilty of?

    Was there any justification for it?

2. What was the root problem here?

3. The Bible says Moses was a humble man. Define humility.

4. How does the Lord respond to the criticisms of Miriam and Aaron?

5. Describe a critical spirit.

6. Define correction.

    Which one, criticism or correction, will do the most positive good? Why?

7. What was Miriam's punishment?

    Do you think Aaron was punished as well? How?

8. How does it make you feel that the Lord hears the criticism you make against others?

9. Why is the criticism of our spiritual leaders especially dangerous?

    What can criticism lead to?

10. When you are in the middle of criticism, how should you handle it according to Romans 12:17-21 and Colossians 3:12-14?

11. What is the opposite of criticism found in I Thessalonians 5:11?

    Which one would you rather have?

12. When you find yourself tempted to be critical or you feel the actual criticism yourself, ask God to help you let Him handle it. Watch the difference in the results.

LESSON FOUR: RAHAB
Joshua 2, 6:15-25

1. Who was Rahab? Describe her.

2. Why do you think the spies chose Rahab's house to stay in?

3. Why do you think Rahab risked her life for the two men?

4. Have you ever taken risks to be identified as one of God's gals?

5. What did Rahab believe about God?

6. Why is faith a fundamental must in your Christian walk?

7. Nothing happens by coincidence. What was the significance in the scarlet rope?

8. Knowing Rahab's "past," what do you think she would say about the word grace?

How do you feel about that precious word grace?

9. Of all the women in the Old Testament, why do you think Rahab is singled out for special comment, even in the New Testament?

10. The Lord wants you to forget your past (Isaiah 43:18). He forgives and forgets. From Matthew 1:5, what were the far-reaching effects of Rahab's decision?

   Follow Rahab's lineage—to whom does it lead?

11. What kinds of people can God use to accomplish His purpose?

   How does this affect you?

LESSON FIVE: RUTH AND NAOMI
Ruth 1 - 4

1. This story is a lesson on loyalty. What is loyalty?

    What makes it hard to be loyal to another person?

2. Briefly explain the story in Ruth 1.

3. Describe the character and personality of Ruth.

    How is it different from Orpah's?

4. What were the religious and cultural differences between Ruth and Naomi?

5. Ruth was following God's will. She didn't understand it all, yet she was simply obedient. How do you find God's will for your life?

6. Naomi had a difficult life and to grieve was normal. Do you feel that it can be dangerous when an emotion gets out of control or overcomes you? Explain.

    Who is always the solution?

7. What was Ruth's reputation as a gleaner?

    How was Boaz's concept of her different from her own?

8. Describe how this God-centered love story unfolds.

    How does Psalm 139:16 make you feel?

9. What does Naomi think of Boaz?

    What does this union mean to her?

10. Follow the lineage of Ruth and Boaz. See God's almighty hand.

11. How does this beautiful story of loyalty affect you?

12. Loyalty may be difficult, but from this story, do you think it pays off? Explain.

LESSON SIX: HANNAH
I Samuel 1:1 - 2:11

1. What is your reaction when life does not go as you have planned?

2. Why is Hannah's pain so great?

3. What does she do about it?

   How is this a valuable lesson for you?

4. Do you think that how you handle pain and disappointment reveals anything about your faith? Explain.

5. Eli told Hannah to "go in peace." What is real peace? By whom is it produced?

6. What is the perfect formula for peace?

7. Why is it important to give thanks in all circumstances (I Thessalonians 5:18)?

   What does Paul say about giving thanks in Philippians 4:4-7?

8. In order to praise God, do we have to know the answer immediately? Explain.

9. How did Hannah's prayer change her?

10. What did Hannah believe about God? (There are several things.)

    · Do you think her beliefs helped her in her actions and attitude?

11. Hannah kept her promise. She committed her son to the Lord's service. How do our actions prove our heart condition?

12. What did you learn from Hannah about the solution to the pain of your unfulfilled hopes and dreams?

LESSON SEVEN: ABIGAIL
I Samuel 25:2-44

1.   Describe Abigail and her situation.

2.   What is a fool? (Psalm 14:1).

3.   What was David's request?

4.   What was Nabal's response?

     What was David's response?

5.   Abigail, being no fool, went to work. What did she do to get ready?

     What was the servant's attitude toward her?

6.   David was very angry. Do you think anger can get out of hand? Explain. (Proverbs 29:11, Ephesians 4:26, James 1:20.)

     How could "out-of-control anger" have changed the course of David's life?

7.   When Abigail met David, how did she treat him?

     What helped him snap back to his senses?

8. Describe Abigail's return to Nabal.

9. Abigail demonstrated amazing calm, humbleness, gentleness, and great wisdom. How did she accomplish all of that? (Isaiah 30:15,21; Jeremiah 17:7-8; Hebrews 4:16.)

10. The Lord has a way of handling wrongs perfectly. How does He handle Nabal?

11. How does the Lord bless Abigail?

12. Praise the Lord that Romans 8:28-30 is absolutely true.

LESSON EIGHT: THE SHUNAMMITE WOMAN
II Kings 4:8-37

1. What do you know about the Shunammite woman from this passage? Describe her.

2. How did she use what she had to help Elisha and his servant?

   How do you think that affects Elisha?

3. How important is hospitality? Explain.

   Do you need to have a supply of endless resources to show it?

4. Elisha wanted to say thank you in some special way. What was her response?

   What insight did Gehazi have?

5. From verses 16-20, what happened?

6. Did that make any sense? Why or why not?

   Do you feel that sometimes God's plan for your life does not make sense? Does He have to?

7. Define the sovereignty of God.

8. Why is it important to lay a foundation of faith and trust in God before times of crisis?

9. What is discipline (Hebrews 12:11)?

    Who does the Lord discipline (Proverbs 3:11-12)?

    How does it "grow us up" in our faith (Hebrews 12:11)?

10. From verses 29-37, tell what Elisha did.

11. Perfect endings are not always a reality. What are your two choices when you are faced with a not so perfect ending?

12. Pray that the Lord teaches you how to have faith and trust in Him because He does know what He is doing in your life.

LESSON NINE: ESTHER
Esther 1 - 10

1. Read the exciting story of Esther.

2. Who is Esther and what are her uncontrollable circumstances?

   What kind of attitude does Esther have during these times?

3. When Mordecai heard about Haman's plot to kill the Jews, what did he ask Esther to do?

   Why was this such a difficult request for Esther?

4. When Esther showed fear of the rules, what was Mordecai's reply?

   What was Esther's response (4:12-17)?

5. Was Esther drawn out of her comfort zone?

   What does that feel like?

6. Where did Esther get her strength and confidence?

   Where do you get your strength and confidence? (Be honest). Is there a lesson here?

7. How did God work out the fate of Haman and the advancement of Mordecai?

   What lesson is learned by these events?

8. God is love, but God is also just. Explain the justice of God.

9. How are the Jews spared?

   Does that show the king's trust in Esther?

10. It is not always easy to stand up for what is right. How does Galatians 6:9, I Corinthians 15:58, Philippians 4:13,19, and II Timothy 1:7 help you?

LESSON TEN: MARY AND...
Various Scriptures

1. Read Luke 1:26-38. Why do you think Mary was picked for this all-important task?

2. When the situation looked impossible, how did she react?

   What was the angel's response? What was Mary's second response?

3. How can your response to impossible situations be similar to Mary's second response?

4. From John 2:1-5, what changes did Mary have to adjust to?

5. From John 19:25-27, put yourself in Mary's place. Explain your feelings.

6. Read Luke 10:38-42. What was going on here?

   Explain Jesus' words to Martha.

7. From John 11:1-44, why didn't Jesus come right over when He heard that Lazarus was sick?

8. When Jesus arrived in Bethany, who went out to meet him?

   How do we know that Martha was changed?

9. Why did Mary hold back?

   Do you think grief can get in the way of what we believe? If so, what happens?

10. In John 4:1-42, the stories of the Samaritan woman and the woman with a sinful past show us that these two gals needed a shot of healthy self-esteem. What are the five steps to achieving that?

11. The sick woman in Mark 5:24-34 was at the end of her rope. Why is that not a bad place to be?

12. Note the contrast between the character of Herodias' daughter and Timothy. Why is your influence so vitally important to eyes that are watching (Matthew 14:1-12, II Timothy 1:1-7)?

13. The influence you want others to see comes from your relationship with Jesus. That comes from Bible study. Do you see now why Bible study should be a part of your everyday schedule? How else are you going to become that Proverbs 31 woman? The Bible IS relevant.